19800

D0355448

FORTRESS
INTRODUCTION TO THE PROPHETS

Library
Oakland S.U.M.

Library
Oakland S.U.M.

FORTRESS
INTRODUCTION TO THE PROPHETS

Rodney R. Hutton

Fortress Press ◆ Minneapolis

FORTRESS INTRODUCTION TO THE PROPHETS

Copyright © 2004 Augsburg Fortress. All rights reserved. Except for brief quotations in critical articles or reviews, no part of this book may be reproduced in any manner without prior written permission from the publisher. Write: Permissions, Augsburg Fortress, Box 1209, Minneapolis, MN 55440-1209.

Cover art: Sand photo © Photodisc, Inc. Other illustrations by Barbara Zuber from *Graphics for Worship 2.0*, copyright © 1999 Augsburg Fortress.

Scripture quotations from the New Revised Standard Version Bible, copyright © 1989 by the Division of Christian Education of the National Council of the Churches of Christ in the USA, are used by permission.

Library of Congress Cataloging-in-Publication Data

Hutton, Rodney R.
  Fortress introduction to the Prophets / Rodney R. Hutton.
    p. cm.
  Includes bibliographical references (p.) and index.
  ISBN 0-8006-3670-8 (alk. paper)
  1. Bible. O.T. Prophets—Criticism, interpretation, etc. 2. Bible. O.T. Jeremiah—Criticism, interpretation, etc. 3. Prophecy—Judaism. I. Title.
  BS1505.52.H48 2004
  224'.061—dc22
                                    2004011404

The paper used in this publication meets the minimum requirements of American National Standard for Information Sciences—Permanence of Paper for Printed Library Materials, ANSI Z329.48-1984.

Manufactured in the U.S.A.
08   07   06   05   04   1   2   3   4   5   6   7   8   9   10

CONTENTS

Preface

The traditional Jewish collection of scriptures is referred to as the *Tanak*, an abbreviation representing its three major divisions: the Law (*torah*), the Prophets (*nebi'im*), and the Writings (*ketubim*). Included in the collection of these prophetic books are those that Christians traditionally have regarded as history rather than prophecy—the books of Joshua, Judges, Samuel, and Kings, the so-called Former Prophets. Conversely, the Christian tradition has included Daniel among the prophetic books, but in the Jewish canon Daniel is included not in the *nebi'im* but rather in the *ketubim*, the Writings.

The reason for these variances is complex and will only be hinted at in chapter 1 of our study. But the very fact that the books of Joshua through Kings can be considered prophecy in any sense ought to signal the reader that caution is warranted when considering what is meant in the first place when we speak of prophecy. If the book of 2 Kings, for example, is prophecy, then certainly whatever is meant by the term goes far beyond a simple reference to fortune-telling and prognostication. Prophecy is in some sense a declaration of the future, but the prophetic oracles of the Old Testament do not have as their *primary* referent some event lying centuries after the word. The prophetic message is directed toward the immediacy of divine action, toward the current unfolding of divine activity that impinges even on the present. Furthermore, in some sense prophecy is not fundamentally about the future at all but, as attested in the books of Joshua through Kings, has to do with how the past is understood and appropriated. If the books of Joshua through Kings are in some sense prophetic, then conversely the books of Isaiah through Malachi are, in an equal sense, historical. They reveal to us God's salvific purposes at work in the history of ancient Israel.

This brief introduction to the prophetic literature of the Old Testament begins with the premise that Israel's prophets had to do as much with the past and the present as with the future. If we look for analogues to the prophetic figures of ancient Israel, we might find them in television commentators or newspaper editorialists, those who scan current events and, based upon trajectories of historical currents, draw out implications for the immediate future. It is fundamentally an abuse of the integrity of ancient prophetic texts to rummage through them and co-opt bits and pieces as evidence for current events in the twenty-first century, as widespread a practice as this might be. This volume seeks above all else to understand the message of the prophets within the context of their own past and present situations, understanding their message to be directed to the immediacy of conflicted and critical events contemporary with the prophets themselves.

This book begins by laying out some fundamental characteristics of prophecy and then considers Israel's preexilic prophets in roughly chronological order. Because of the importance of the prophets Isaiah and Jeremiah in this material, these books are given somewhat closer attention, especially that of Jeremiah. It is hoped that, although missing here is a discussion of Israel's exilic and postexilic prophets, leading to the apocalyptic book of Daniel, this study will nevertheless serve to introduce the reader to the critical issues that concern Israel's prophetic texts in their broad scope. One can hope that the gap in attention to the exilic and postexilic texts might soon be remedied. Most of the biblical citations are quoted from the NRSV (New Revised Standard Version of the Bible), but when not they are my own translations aimed at more literally rendering the underlying Hebrew text. The lack of footnotes will undoubtedly distract those who wish for a closer control of evidence but will, I hope, enhance the reading for those for whom the volume is intended—those who are, for the first time, encountering Israel's prophetic literature in a serious study or who wish to regain a familiarity with the "forest" so that they can once again slug their way through the "trees" of weekly lectionary texts.

I wish to thank the Evangelical Lutheran Church of Russia and Other States (ELKRAS) and its seminary in Novosaratovka, near St. Petersburg, for providing the occasion for formalizing this overview of prophetic literature in conjunction with a period spent teaching there in 2003. The students at Novosaratovka can perhaps be thankful themselves that, given the practical situation in the classroom, I did not read to them from the manuscripts but rather closed the lecture notes and simply "had at it." I would also like to thank my class of students at Trinity Lutheran Seminary during this last winter quarter who were first exposed to these chapters in their introductory course of study. None of them seem to have suffered irrevocably from the exposure, and I can only hope that one or two might have caught a bug for further investigation.

CHAPTER 1

Introduction to
Old Testament Prophecy

◆

Five Questions to Begin Our Study

Those who study Israel's prophetic literature will invariably bring their own questions and insights with them as they approach the biblical text. In the current conversation, however, scholars have posed a number of questions that have fundamentally shaped the debate, questions about both significant details and larger perspectives. We need to begin our review of the topic by considering, even if only briefly, these larger perspectival questions that are critical for moving forward into a more detailed study.

The first question concerns the fact that the literary character of the prophetic books gives them a quality at considerable distance from the quality and perspective of the oracles recorded either in the historical books of the Old Testament or Hebrew Bible (i.e., the Deuteronomistic History of Joshua, Judges, 1–2 Samuel, and 1–2 Kings) or in prophetic texts found by archaeologists throughout the ancient Near East. Given such a variance between the literary quality of the biblical prophetic books and the phenomenon of Near Eastern and Israelite prophecy that scholars have reconstructed, the first and most basic question is this: Do the prophetic books witness at all to a real phenomenon of "prophecy" in Israel? Today many scholars suggest that the persons whom we meet in the books of the various prophets are far removed from what a real prophet would have looked like in ancient Israel. A good case is that of Amos, who almost certainly rejected being called a prophet (*nabi'*). Amos insists that he was a sheep breeder and fruit grower, and disclaims being a prophet (Amos 7:12-15). Another case is that of the prophet Jeremiah. Though Jeremiah never disclaims the prophetic office, some scholars—especially those following the lead of the Greek text of the book—have raised the question of whether he would have accepted the professional designation or rejected it. Was he really a prophet, or was he a poet, only to be resculpted into a prophet by later editors or redactors? Some scholars insist that Jeremiah hated prophets and would never have accepted the title for himself. It was, according to this view, only a later tradition—represented by the Masoretic text, or received Hebrew text—that turned Jeremiah into a prophet, placing upon him "the mantle of Elijah."

It is clear that the long and baroquely expanded prose and poetic oracles that are recorded in the prophetic books do not look very similar to the terse and crisply written oracles that have survived in ancient prophetic texts uncovered in various places in the Near East. Given what might be the result more of a literary effort than a historical attempt to preserve an actual historical phenomenon, how close can we get to the phenomenon of prophecy by studying the books of the *nebi'im*, the title given the collection of prophetic books in the Hebrew Bible? One must always be cautious about assuming that the prophetic books give a literal and accurate portrayal of the phenomenon of prophecy in ancient Israel.

Second, there is a related question concerning the inner-biblical evidence itself. What is the relationship of the classical or writing prophets (those to whom books are ascribed) to the preclassical prophets, about whom we read in the prophetic legends preserved in the Deuteronomistic History? How does the phenomenon of prophecy as represented by the book of Jeremiah, for example, relate to the type of prophetic office or profession as demonstrated in the legendary accounts about Elijah or Elisha, reported by the Deuteronomistic Historian? Is the relationship of Elijah to Jeremiah primarily continuous or discontinuous? Do the figures of Nathan and Ahijah the Shilonite give expression to the same social institution as those of Isaiah and Ezekiel, or is there such a transformation of Israelite prophecy before the writing prophets that we lose any meaningful way to compare or contrast the two phenomena?

Another aspect of this "inner-biblical" consideration is that the Deuteronomistic Historian seems interested in the prophetic movement for his own reasons and purposes, and uses the traditions selectively and ideologically. Contrast, for example, the portrait of Isaiah in 2 Kings 19, where he functions simply as a salvific prophet assuring Judeans of divine protection against the invading Assyrians, with that of the prophet Isaiah in Isaiah 1–5, where his message is aligned much more directly with the hard-hitting judgment oracles of Amos. Was the Deuteronomistic Historian unfamiliar with the traditions of the early Isaiah? Or did he suppress those traditions for polemical reasons? More generally, why is the Deuteronomistic Historian nearly silent with regard to the writing prophets, focusing instead on collections of prophetic narratives about persons otherwise unknown from the prophetic corpus: Nathan, Gad, Ahijah of Shiloh, Elijah, Elisha, and so on? Of the writing prophets, the Deuteronomistic Historian mentions only two: Isaiah and Jonah. Even his treatment of Jonah, however, is limited to a brief biographical note in 2 Kings 14:25 relating the oracles of Jonah to the political expansionism of Jeroboam II.

Third, where are we to find the origins of Israelite prophecy? Initially, it is tempting to assume that prophecy is an exclusively Israelite and biblical phenomenon. But is this true? What are the roots of biblical prophecy and in what other ancient Near Eastern cultures do we find similar phenomena? The clearest connection seems to be that of the so-called Mari prophets, who appear to us from ancient texts discovered by archaeologists at the city of Mari on the upper Euphrates River. Indeed, in these prophetic texts from Mari, dating to approximately 1775 B.C.E., fully a thousand years before the biblical text began to take shape, we meet several different types of prophets or "spokespersons for the gods," some called *apilu*, some called *muhhu*. But they all serve to bring a revealed message from a god to the king of Mari. What can we learn about such ancient Near Eastern forms of prophecy, and what do they tell us about the origins of prophecy in Israel?

Fourth, how do the prophets relate to their culture and society? What is their relationship to the local temple and its worship life and cultic practice, to the institution of kingship and the local leadership, and to other religious traditions celebrated by the community? Are the prophets primarily voices of social cohesion, trying to hold society together by calling it back to central core values? Or are they voices of social disruption, opposed to the king and the temple, working to "pluck up, pull down, destroy, and overthrow," to use the words of the prophet Jeremiah? And what is the relationship between prophecy and wider forms of divination, such as those performed by the priests in Israel and throughout the wider ancient Near East?

This problem of social location is confounded by the fact that several different technical terms are used to identify prophets in the Old Testament writings. We read of persons called visionaries (*hozeh*), seers (*ro'eh*), prophets (*nabi'*), and men of God (*'ish 'elohim*). Did these various titles refer to the same social phenomenon? Would a *hozeh*, for example, have understood himself to be identical to a *nabi'*, or would the two have understood themselves differently? How many variant forms of prophecy are reflected in the Old Testament? First Samuel 9:9 certainly indicates that popular usage of such technical terms shifted over time, and that the term seer had fallen out of usage by the time of the composition of the Deuteronomistic History (ca. 600 to 550 B.C.E.). But the text of Amos 7:12-14 further confounds this problem: Amaziah refers to Amos as a visionary (*hozeh*), but Amos responds, "I am not a prophet (*nabi'*)." Were the terms already interchangeable by the mid-eighth century B.C.E.? What are the original social locations represented by persons carrying these various titles?

The fifth and final question concerns the canonical structure of the biblical text and the relationship of the prophetic corpus to the larger collection of Sacred Scripture. How does the prophetic collection of writings relate to the legal and historical traditions of Israel, that is, to the Torah of Moses and to the historical writings produced by both the Deuteronomist (Joshua, Judges, 1-2 Samuel, and 1-2 Kings) and the Chronicler (1-2 Chronicles, Ezra, and Nehemiah)? What is the significance of the fact that the books of the Deuteronomistic History, unlike those of the Chronicler, are regarded as a part of the prophetic canon in Judaism and the Hebrew Bible (the "former prophets")? How does the canonical process affect how one interprets the prophets (e.g., Isaiah of Jerusalem in relation to Second and Third Isaiah; Zechariah in relation to Second Zechariah; the collection of the twelve minor prophets in one scroll)? Further, what is the relation between the prophets and the Law? Are the prophets the creative genius behind Israel's religious development and its ethical monotheism? Or do they simply reflect a long-standing ethos and repeat the tradition that they have inherited?

These questions are fundamentally insoluble, but they must be borne in mind as we consider the prophetic writings in closer detail. They provide the larger investigative framework within which any study of the prophets must be undertaken.

Judaism: The Prophets as Guardians of the Torah

Up to modern times there have been three characteristic ways of viewing the prophets. Judaism has tended to regard the prophets as traditionalists, as those who have kept the tradition of the Mosaic Torah and have passed it down through the generations. Judaism always understood the Torah to be the heart of the faith and regarded the prophets as bearing witness to the Law. Even today, the chief reading in Jewish synagogues is the Torah reading, and it is supplemented by a reading from the Prophets, the haftarah reading, that is understood to accompany the Torah reading and comment on it or give it a particular application. The prophets, in this model, are understood to serve the Torah, to stand under its constitutive guidance. This placing of the prophets under the authority of the Torah is clearly at work already in Deuteronomistic theology. Consider Deuteronomy 18:15, when Moses tells the people before entering the promised land: "A prophet from your midst, from among your own brothers, like me, will Yahweh your God raise up for you." Moses becomes the prototype of the prophet, whose basic mission is to deliver to the people the Torah of God, delivered to them on Mount Sinai. This Mosaic role of the prophet, characteristic of the Deuteronomistic History, is summed up in 2 Kings 17:13: "yet Yahweh warned Israel and Judah by every prophet and every seer, saying, 'Turn from your evil ways and keep my commandments and my statutes, in accordance with all the law that I commanded your ancestors and that I sent to you by my servants the prophets.'"

Christianity: The Prophets as Foretellers of Christ

If Judaism has tended to understand the prophets as guardians of the Torah, Christianity has tended to understand the prophets as foretellers of Christ. This is clear from the way the New Testament searches the prophetic writings for prophecies that it understands to predict the birth, life, death, and resurrection of Jesus. Sometimes the New Testament writers were obvious about it—like Matthew, who repeatedly informs the reader "such and such happened in order to fulfill what was spoken by the prophets" (Matt 1:22; 2:15; 8:17; 12:17; 13:35; 21:4; 26:56). At other times the writers are more subtle, but one can easily see that an event is regarded as "fulfilling scripture." Consider the case of Elisha's feeding miracle (2 Kgs 4:42-44) as a prototype of the popular feeding miracle of Jesus reported in the Gospels. The prophetic writings were like the various colors of paint on the palette of the Gospel artist as he set about to paint his portrait of Jesus Christ. The prophetic corpus was the source of inspiration of the Gospel writers, much more so than was the Torah of Moses. Not surprisingly, the Christian lectionary readings concentrate much more on sections from the Old Testament prophets than on passages from the books of Moses, even though as children it was stories from Genesis and Exodus that fed us. But it is as though when we became adult Christians we had to abandon those stories and turn instead to the prophets, where we imagined that the real message of the Old Testament was heard.

Above, I mentioned Moses' words in Deuteronomy 18:15, which promises that in each generation a prophet shall be raised up for the people to pass on to them the Torah of Moses. But in Christianity it was important to understand this text in the light of Deuteronomy 34:10, where the narrator says, "Never again (*lo'. . . 'od*) did a prophet rise up in Israel like Moses, whom Yahweh knew face-to-face." But this "never again" (*lo'. . . 'od*) was eventually taken in the late Old Testament tradition to mean "not yet," and there developed a heightened sense of expectation that some day such a prophet would indeed arise. The church read Deuteronomy 18:15 through the lens of Deuteronomy 34:10 and then as refracted through the prism of Malachi 3:1-2, in which God promises, "See, I am sending my messenger [the name Malachi means 'my messenger'] to prepare the way before me." The New Testament, then, understands the text in Malachi to refer to the inauguration of the Christ event. Matthew 11:10, for example, takes the reference in Malachi to refer to John the Baptist. There Matthew's Jesus says, "This [John the Baptist] is the one about whom it is written, 'See, I am sending my messenger ahead of you, who will prepare your way before you.'" This trajectory from Deuteronomy 18:15 to

Deuteronomy 34:10 to Malachi 3:1-2 and then to the New Testament was critical in shaping the way Christianity came to regard the prophets.

Liberal Protestantism: The Prophets as Bearer's of Israel's Truth

So Judaism understood the prophets to be the guardians of the Torah while Christianity took the prophets to be foretellers of the Christ event. But the conversation took an interesting direction in the nineteenth century, shaped by the Western romanticism on one hand and by Western Hegelianism and science on the other. Under the influence of the spirit of romanticism, which swept over European culture in the early nineteenth century, the prophets came to represent the noble human spirit freed from social constraints, unchained from oppressive social institutions. The "noble savage," idealized in romantic ideology by the writings of the eighteenth-century philosopher Jean-Jacques Rousseau, came to serve as the model by which the prophets were understood: brave anti-institutional spokespersons for God who were untainted by society's poisonous stain, free to stare kings and priests in the face and reject their formal and polite social conventions.

But nineteenth-century philosophy and science, and especially Hegelianism and Darwinism, also affected the liberal-critical view of the prophets, especially in the work of the German scholar Julius Wellhausen. One of Wellhausen's great dictums was that, instead of the prophets coming after the Law and being the guardians and representatives of the Law, they in fact come before the Law. Wellhausen was a nineteenth-century Protestant scholar attempting to write a history of Israel. To do so, however, he realized that he needed to understand the historical contexts of the various biblical sources. In order to lay out his understanding of the historical context of the pentateuchal sources, he wrote a book entitled *Prolegomena to the History of Israel*, in which he analyzed the sources and developed the now famous "Documentary Hypothesis" of the writing of the Pentateuch (the well-known J, E, D, and P sources): the Yahwistic material was dated to the period of the Solomonic enlightenment in Judah, the Elohistic material to a bit later in the north (Israel), the Deuteronomic material to a period a couple of generations before or else associated with the reform movement of Josiah (ca. 620 B.C.E.), and the Priestly material dated last, to the period after the exile during the restoration of the Judean community under the leadership of Ezra (ca. 500–400 B.C.E.). Since the prophets are associated in general with the Deuteronomic movement, and since the Law is associated with the Priestly material, one can see why Wellhausen coined the expression that "the Prophets (D) come before the Law (P)."

Many of Wellhausen's conclusions still stand today, though nothing has been left unmodified. His work has had a tremendous impact on scholarship. One of the resulting difficulties, however, is the way his conclusions hardened the Christian and specifically Protestant understanding of how it is that the prophets function in relation to the Law: not as a commentary on the Law (so the Jewish position) but rather as standing over against the Law. According to this view, not only were the prophets first (i.e., before the Law)—they were the real geniuses in creating a new theological expression, labeled in the nineteenth and twentieth centuries as ethical monotheism. Hard-core Wellhausians, and most Protestants, understood the prophets to be the font and source of Israel's, and the church's, faith. As such, the Law came to be even further devalued in Christian and Protestant circles. It came to be regarded as even *less* than a commentary on the prophets. Indeed, it came to stand over *against* the prophets. In this hard-core Wellhausian perspective, the prophets came to represent the prior truth of God's word for the world and the Law came to represent a later accretion, a relatively late and degenerate form of religious expression focused on trivial minutiae concerning ritual purity, sacrifices, food laws, and the like. The Law was regarded as the anti-gospel that had perverted the earlier and pure word of the prophets, an anti-gospel that Jesus had to dismantle in order to restore the pristine gospel of ethical monotheism.

Concluding Comments

The impact of romanticism and evolutionary science on the study of the prophets has contributed to our misunderstanding of Israel's prophets since the nineteenth century. If the effect of the church's theology was to cut the prophets loose from their tether to the Mosaic Torah, the effect of nineteenth- and twentieth-century critical scholarship has been to set them at odds with their connection to Israel's fundamental faith as expressed in the Torah, to turn the two into enemies of one another. It is far too simple to blame Wellhausen for the full expression of anti-Semitism as it emerged in Nazi Germany and continues in the world today. But we must be aware that even seemingly safe theological conversations can have dramatic effects on how we view the world and others around us. While scholars today generally accept the major lines of Wellhausen's argument concerning the development of Israel's theological traditions (though not without considerable debate and rethinking specific issues), there is a welcome movement away from a simple evolutionary scheme of interpreting Israel's confessional development. Scholars today resist the notion that the prophets can be so easily co-opted by a prophetically inspired church or society to point exclusively to Jesus and not first and foremost to Israel's own historical and social situation. There is also strong resistance to the idea that the prophets can be used in our conversations to make claims about Judaism being a degeneration of true biblical faith or to excommunicate Judaism from its position in God's mysterious course of salvation.

In the next chapter, we turn to look at the origins of the prophetic movement in Israel and consider its first great exponent—the prophet Amos.

CHAPTER 2

The Origins of Israelite Prophecy and Amos

◆

The Forms of Old Testament Prophecy

It is tempting for the casual reader to think that prophecy is a uniquely Israelite religious phenomenon. In fact, however, every ancient society and most modern ones express the need for the human realm to be able to communicate with the divine realm or with transcendent power. Sometimes this need for communication took the form of an official state-supported institution associated with royal sanctuaries. At other times this communication took a freer form by which "freelance" prophets would find markets for their services apart from state-supported sanctuaries. In addition to the intuitive visions experienced by prophetic figures, such divine-human intermediation would also take the form of divination in which physical materials would be manipulated or examined by experts for information, such as the inspection of animal livers or the throwing of arrows. In Israel the early use of sacral lots or dice, called Urim and Thummim (Hebrew *'urim* and *tummim*), was a form of divination, or the manipulation and examination of physical objects. Although it may seem strange or even improper, we should also place in this same category the consultation and study of texts, whether the manuals on liver inspection used in Babylon or the priestly codes and manuals used in Israel for settling disputes or determining levels of impurity or sanctity. So in Israel, the priest was the one who used the Urim and Thummim in order to obtain divine information, and it was also the priest who was responsible for "Torah," that is, for the preservation of Israel's legal traditions.

These two forms of intermediation—the intuitive and the divinatory—were not mutually exclusive, but were used in tandem with one another as cross-checks to ascertain transcendent information or the divine will, both in Israel and in the wider world. An interesting example of this interrelationship between the intuitive and the divinatory is the sort of prophecy that we find at the ancient Mesopotamian city of Mari, where several different types of prophets are described, among which were the *muhhu* (ecstatic) and the *apilu* (dispenser of oracles). A collection of prophetic texts from Mari depicts how prophetic messages were received by these Mari prophets while visiting a temple or sanctuary. Upon witnessing such a prophetic oracle, the priest in charge of the sanctuary would then record the prophecy and send it, along with a piece of the prophet's hair or clothing, to the king, together with instructions that the king should have his own diviners put the hair and piece of cloth to some sort of test in order to determine whether the oracle was true and whether it should be given serious consideration by the king or dismissed as wrong or inconsequential. This social phenomenon at Mari shows the interplay between the intuitive form of intermediation, by which a prophet receives a vision or audition of a divine word, and the divinatory form of intermediation, by which the royal experts would examine physical data as hard evidence to determine an aspect of the truth.

Israel, too, knew of a number of ways of receiving divine information, whether by dreams or visions, Urim and Thummim, divination, or necromancy (consultation with the deceased). Consider the famous case of 1 Samuel 28:6ff., which narrates the account of Saul's attempt to gain divine information by dreams, by Urim and Thummim, by prophets, but to no avail. None of these forms of intermediation was effective. So he resorted to a means that he himself had declared to be illegal: necromancy. In Israel there were different names for such "experts": the *hozeh* was one who had visionary experiences; the *ro'eh* was one who was clairvoyant and could see into the future or into remote locations; the *qosem* was one who divined by various methods; the *nabi'* was one who was called by God; there was the person who was thought to be possessed by or to possess something called an *'ob*, the power by which the dead could be conjured and asked questions.

The practice of necromancy has been taken by some to explain the connection between the action of "inquiry" (*sha'al*) and the realm of the dead (*she'ol*). Eventually these various forms of prophecy and intermediation were either outlawed (like necromancy), fell out of use (like Urim and Thummim), or were joined together into a larger category. As noted above, for example, we are told in 1 Samuel 9:9: "Formerly in Israel, anyone who went to inquire of God would say, 'Come, let us go to the seer'; for the one who is now called a prophet was formerly called a seer."

As at Mari, where the temple priest had control and oversight of the prophets who received oracles at his sanctuary, so in Israel the temple priests also seem to have had oversight and control of the prophets. The book of Amos relates the story, for example, of the prophet Amos being expelled from the royal sanctuary at Bethel by the priestly overseer Amaziah. Similarly, we learn from the book of Jeremiah how Jeremiah was arrested by the priest Pashhur, the "chief officer in the house of the Lord" (20:1-6); and in Jeremiah 29:26 we learn that there was apparently an "officer in the house of the Lord to control any madman who plays the prophet, to put him in the stocks and the collar." Priests and prophets functioned in tandem with one another in a complex process of determining the will of God for how the king should conduct the daily business of the state. That the buck had to stop somewhere, however, and that this final authority was lodged with the priest, would inevitably lead to conflicts between temple priests and those prophets who used the temple as the place for receiving and dispensing oracles. Such priestly oversight of the prophets could lead to conflicts between them, and apparently often did.

The Development of Israelite Prophecy

The Deuteronomistic History presents an interesting window upon the early forms of prophecy that were current in ancient Israelite society. So we read about Samuel the "clairvoyant" in 1 Samuel 9:6-9, who is called a "man of God" and a "seer," and who can "see" where Saul's family donkeys are. In 10:5-13 we meet the band of prophets who are playing their instruments and engaged in a "prophetic frenzy," which, when they are met by King Saul, sweeps Saul up into the frenzy too, so that he is "possessed by the spirit of Yahweh and turned into another man." Such a frenzy, we learn in 19:24, can cause one to strip off one's clothes and roll naked on the ground all night long, as it did Saul himself.

But in addition to these orgiastic forms of prophetic experience, we also meet the figures of Nathan, Gad, Ahijah of Shiloh, Jonah, and the hundreds of prophets who worked at the royal court. These prophets seemed to function much more calmly, without wild ecstatic outbursts and naked fits. They seemed to function more like royal advisors, meeting with the king to review strategy or to reveal divine promises or divine punishments, pronouncing dynastic oracles or retracting them, giving words of victory to the king about to set out on a military campaign or giving warnings of defeat. To draw a strict distinction between the phenomenon of orgiastic and ecstatic prophecy on one hand and a more rational, calm, and orderly form on the other is dangerous, however, and it is doubtful that any such professional distinction existed. It is always tempting for us to assume that true prophets always acted rationally and calmly, in line with how we imagine royal advisors should act given our own social conventions. Saul and his ecstatic band of prophets, we might think, are easily relegated to the ranks of marginalized religious fanatics, who should be institutionalized rather given serious credence for their oracles. But it is likely that even the calmest-appearing prophet in Israel was no less ecstatic than was Saul and the band of prophets. So we are a bit surprised and shocked to learn from Isaiah 20:2-3 that Isaiah himself walked around naked for three years! Of course we know that Jeremiah engaged in many peculiar prophetic actions, and Ezekiel did so many strange things that modern readers have often assumed that he must have suffered from some sort of chronic mental or physical illness. Recall the comment made above regarding the temple priest in Jeremiah who was said to have control of any madman (*meshugga'*; 29:26) who plays the prophet. It was commonly believed that the line between prophetic inspiration and insanity was a fine one indeed.

The exact origins of prophecy in Israel are impossible to determine. Scholars commonly speak of the phenomenon of "war prophecy" as at least one of the early forms, alongside that of the clairvoyance of Samuel and the court advising of Nathan, Gad, and Ahijah. War prophecy was the phenomenon of prophets and diviners that not only indicated whether a particular military campaign would be successful or fail but also included the prophet's more direct involvement in cursing the enemies and fanning the flames of passion and resolve in the hearts of the soldiers. An illustration of this war prophecy is the figure of Balaam in Numbers 22–24, who is hired by King Balaak to "curse Israel" as they move through the wilderness toward the land of Canaan. Another example is that of the prophet Elisha, who, in 2 Kings 13:15-19, uses an arrow ritual to indicate that Israel will defeat the Aramaeans—but only three times. Similarly, we read in 2 Kings 14:25 that the prophet Jonah was instrumental in securing a victory of Israel under Jeroboam II over their enemies at Lebo-hamath. In this same category falls the story of Micaiah ben Imlah and the four hundred prophets of Ahab in 1 Kings 22, which tells of court prophets encouraging the king to go forth to battle and assuring victory. Whether or not it was the particular context of warfare in which prophetic experience came to such importance, it is clear that prophecy played out its major social function within the context of the royal court.

Amos, the Prophet from Tekoa

Amos is the earliest of the so-called writing prophets and is the most brutally unforgiving. There is less hope for the future expressed in Amos than in any other prophetic book, and the book of Amos is almost completely expressed as a judgment oracle of coming destruction. At best the prophet can conjure up painful admonitions for Israel to "seek Yahweh and live" (5:4-6), but there is little hope and even less comfort. The leaders of Israel seem incapable of responding to God. They cannot even respond to God's repeated chastising correction—famine, drought, blight and mildew, pestilence, military disaster (4:6-11). Doom and gloom fill the pages of the book until the very end, where just a few scant verses surprisingly give way to a final slim ray of light and hope that the "fallen booth of David" will be repaired and rebuilt, a day "when the plowman shall overtake the reaper and the treader of grapes him who sows the seed; the mountains shall drip sweet wine and all the hills shall flow with it" (9:11-15). Up to this point, however, the book of Amos is almost totally an unrelenting series of judgment oracles promising only ruin and destruction.

Unlike Hosea, who will shortly follow Amos and who focuses on the religious matters of the pure worship of Yahweh in the face of religious apostasy and Baal worship, Amos seems totally uninterested in such religious concerns. As will soon be demonstrated, for Hosea the problem is Baal worship. For Amos, however, the problem is not Baal worship—there is not a single reference to Baal in the book. Amos seems to be totally unaware that anyone in Israel ever uttered the name Baal. Amos presumes that everyone worships only Yahweh, everywhere and at every time. Indeed, Amos suggests that the people *love* to worship Yahweh. At least they love the ostentatious slathering of sacrifices on the altars of Bethel and Gilgal (Amos 4:4-5). Though the people presume to love such celebrations, underneath their pretense is a callous disregard for such occasions and a wish only that such festival days would hurry to a close so that they could resume their cheating and corruption (8:4-6). Thus Amos focuses on issues of social justice, especially the justice that is being denied the poor by those who are wealthy. The *problem* for Amos is not religious apostasy. It is how one relates the worship of Yahweh to how one lives out one's life with justice and mercy for all, especially for the poor and the most vulnerable members of society.

Amos's Oracles against the Nations

This focus on social justice begins already in the first two chapters, commonly referred to as the "oracles against the nations." Israel's neighbors are not condemned for religious perversion—even neighbors such as Ammon, which worshiped the god Milcom (1 Kgs 11:5, 33; Jer 49:1), or Moab, which worshiped the god Chemosh (Num 21:29; 1 Kgs 11:7, 33; Jer 48:13). They are rather condemned for issues of social justice, for "ripping up women with child" in their rush for conquest of land (Amos 1:13), or for "burning to lime the bones of the king of Edom" (2:1).

Lest the people of Israel begin to take delight in these oracles against their enemies, however, the entire focus of these opening oracles against the nations rests on where they eventually fall: on judgment against Israel itself. First Damascus to the northeast (1:3), then Gaza to the southwest (1:6), then Tyre to the northwest (1:9), then Edom to the southeast (1:11): with such bold strokes, the crosshairs of divine judgment establish the grid upon which the drama will be played out. But then the narrow scope is intensified as the bull's-eye is revealed: Ammon and Moab, the near neighbors to the east, are targeted (1:13; 2:1). Finally Judah is in the gunsight (2:4). But then the chauvinistic thirst for the destruction of the enemies yields to the awful truth that, all along, the crosshairs have been fixed on Israel

(2:6) for selling the righteous for silver and the needy for a pair of shoes, for trampling the head of the poor into the dust of the earth and turning aside the justice of the afflicted (2:6-8). As in all prior cases, God "will not revoke the punishment" (*lo' 'ashibennu*, literally "I will not cause it to return"). That is, God will allow the drama to play itself out—the drama that ensues when one unleashes violent actions and those actions invariably come back upon one's own head in the form of natural consequence or retribution.

Israel's Descent to Death

The central theme is pursued in chapters 3–4 in a scathing attack on the indolence, greed, and corruption of the wealthy classes during this period of Israel's history, generally associated with the period of prosperity and expanding economy during the days of Jeroboam II, about 760 B.C.E. Jeroboam II had the exceptionally good fortune of living during days of Assyrian weakness, when both Israel and Judah were left relatively alone to pursue their own expansionist agendas, raking in international wealth at the expense of the increasing impoverishment and oppression of their own poor. One can hear the emotion born out of righteous anger over this increasing chasm developing between the wealthy and the poor when Amos launches a direct attack against "you cows of Bashan . . . who oppress the poor and crush the needy" (4:1). But such social injustice will lead to their own ruination as those privileged few "lie upon beds of ivory and stretch themselves out upon their couches, eating lambs from the flock and calves from the midst of the stall . . . who drink wine in bowls and anoint themselves with the finest oils, but are not grieved over the ruin of Joseph" (6:4-6). Those indolently wealthy will face divine judgment, and the "first" of all shall be the "first" to go into exile (6:7). The "cream of the crop," so to speak, will get creamed.

In a turn of expression playing on the image of these "fat cows" sleeping on their ivory beds and couches, Amos levels a devastating threat against them in 3:12: "Thus says the Lord: 'As the shepherd rescues from the mouth of the lion two legs or a piece of an ear, so shall the people of Israel who dwell in Samaria be rescued, with the corner of a couch and a post of a bed.'" This is no rescue! This is the salvaging of a few miserly scraps from the mouth of the lion, scraps of what once had been the very marks of their indolent wealth, the symbols of their offense. But who is the lion? The reader has already been told at the beginning of the book: "Yahweh roars from Zion and utters his voice from Jerusalem. The pastures of the shepherds mourn, and the top of Carmel withers" (1:2). "The lion has roared; who will not fear? The Lord God has spoken; who can but prophesy?" (3:8).

This word of pending death and destruction takes the form of a funeral dirge in chapters 5 and 6. "Hear this word that I take up over you in dirge (*qinah*), O house of Israel." Then in the clear death-march meter of Hebrew *qinah* poetry, the poet goes on: "Fallen, no more to rise, is the virgin Israel." It is as though the oracles in these chapters came with a thick black border marked around the edges of the letter. The funeral drums can be heard beating as the coach bearing the casket processes slowly down the street. The meaning is unmistakable. Even the call for Israel to "seek Yahweh and live" comes in the midst of a funeral service, as the casket is being lowered into the ground. This setting gives way to the "woeful" cry "*hoy*" beginning in 5:18 and continuing through chapter 6. The stench of death saturates this material, as the reader is presented the image of a minyan of men (ten), the minimum required for formal worship, gathered together for their own funeral. A rare survivor will be too terrified even to mention the name of Yahweh (6:9-10). This stench of death is matched only by the stench of Israel's burning sacrifices, which Yahweh loathes. Yahweh will not tolerate such stench, nor will God easily be entertained by the noise of Israel's songs. The only offering that Yahweh desires is justice and righteousness, flowing down like torrents of refreshing water (5:21-24).

Amos among the Prophets

As we learn in chapter 7, Amos was probably not a professional prophet by trade, but rather a breeder of sheep and a fruit farmer from a small town in Judah. Amos describes himself as a "herdsman" (*boqer*, 7:14), indicating that he was not a simple shepherd but was rather a rancher engaging in animal husbandry on a larger scale. This suggestion is supported by the reference in 1:1 to Amos being "among the sheep breeders (*noqedim*)." The only other person to whom the Hebrew Bible attributes this professional designation is Mesha, the king of Moab, who would regularly deliver one hundred thousand lambs to the king of Israel (2 Kgs 3:4). Being no meager shepherd but rather a cattle rancher and breeder of sheep, Amos must have had considerable status among his peers in the small Judean town of Tekoa. However, because he had little status among prophetic groups, and—being Judean—had absolutely no status in the royal sanctuary of Israel, he was evicted from the temple at Bethel. Nevertheless, his word lived on in Israelite tradition.

Amos brought a grim word of judgment and death against one of the greatest kings ever in Israel, the powerful Jeroboam II. Amos's word was not bogged down in religious sentimentality and liturgical language about worshiping the right god. He was focused, rather, on worshiping God rightly. If the people thought that they could "hurry the new moon" so that they could get back to business as usual, trampling on the needy and bringing the poor of the land to a miserable end (8:4-5), and then bring in their sacrifices to Yahweh's temple with pious looks on their faces as if everything were okay, then Amos had a word for them: "Death!" They may not yet realize it, still lying comfortably on their ivory beds during those flush days of Jeroboam II. But they were staring into the grave, and it did not require superhuman vision to see that Israel's casket was being lowered by the ropes. Soon the national dress would be changed, and the dress of the day would be sackcloth and baldness on every head, as though mourning for an only child (8:10).

One can only hope that Amos's word is a word that no generation has to endure. It is, however, a word that every generation needs to hear. God does not easily tolerate the sweet smell of sacrifices drenched with the stench of social injustice and of the oppression of the most vulnerable members of society. But as muted and as limited as it is, a whisper of hope can be heard: even over the sound of funeral dirges and the cry of anguished mourners, one can hear the invitation to "seek Yahweh and live." That is the hope unfurled in the last five verses of the book. Even out of the ashes of our broken lives God will raise up vineyards and gardens, and God's people will once again be planted on their land, and they shall never again be plucked up out of the land that they have been given (9:15).

CHAPTER 3

Hosea

Hosea's Historical Context

What the prophet Hosea has in common with Amos, whom we considered in the last chapter, is that they both address a situation during the prosperous days of Jeroboam II, about the middle of the eighth century B.C.E. Because of a temporary decline in Assyrian imperial power, it was a brief period during which Judah and Israel, along with other small western Asian states, could flex their own muscles and venture forth in their own search for wealth, international business, political expansion, and power. It is in this context of growing wealth and an equally growing division between wealthy and poor that Amos and now Hosea step forth on the stage of prophecy. Both Amos and Hosea were prophets who addressed their messages to the rulers and leaders of the kingdom of Israel in the north. Hosea appeared on the scene some years after Amos, however, and by now the political winds were shifting. Assyria was rising up out of its temporary lethargy, and Israel was about to encounter the decline of its nationhood. As Hosea suggested, the end was not long in coming: a series of coups would eventually lead to the loss of the Galilee in 732 B.C.E. and to the collapse of the entire state at the hands of the Assyrians just ten years later, in 722 B.C.E.

Hosea in Contrast to Amos

Though they were roughly contemporary, in many ways Hosea was the antithesis of Amos. Whereas Amos was from a small rural town in Judah to the south, Hosea was from Israel in the north. Even though the book of Hosea never gives us much information about where Hosea lived and what his occupation was, his oracles are filled with references to northern cities: Samaria, Bethel, Gilgal, Adam, Ramah, Gibeah, and Gilead. Never does he mention any Judean towns. Furthermore, many of his oracles allude to traditions that would have been particularly celebrated in and remembered by people in the north: the stories about Jacob and Esau (Hos 12:3); about Jacob and the encounter with God at the Jabbok River (12:3-4); about Jacob's stay with Laban and his marriage to Rachel (12:12); Israel's settlement traditions; the Deuteronomic theology and traditions about Moses' prophetic office (12:13); the traditions of the Decalogue (4:2). Hosea repeatedly but cryptically rehearses historical memories preserved especially in the north: the bloody coup of Jehu at Jezreel (1:4; cf. 2 Kgs 9:1—10:11); the disastrous theft of Achan at Achor/Ai (2:15; cf. Josh 7:1-26); the Benjaminite offense at Gibeah (9:9; cf. Judg 19:1—20:48); the Assyrian slaughter of the town of Beth-arbel under Shalmaneser (Hos 10:14). All these, together with an absence of traditions relating to David and Abraham, stamp Hosea as a northerner, and one comfortable with the urban traditions of the major centers of power.

The most significant difference between Amos and Hosea, however, is the manner in which they understand the central problem facing Israel. Amos, we saw, was not focused on worshiping the right god, since he never questions that the people are worshiping no other god but Yahweh, the God of Israel. Amos, as was detailed above, focuses rather on worshiping God rightly. Here is a major difference between Amos and his near contemporary, Hosea. Hosea focuses almost exclusively on the question of which god it is that the people are worshiping. Whereas Amos seems to be indifferent to or unaware of Israel's apostate religious practices, Hosea is fixated on them. According to him, Israel is obsessed by a fascination with the Canaanite god Baal as though it were a sexual addiction. Whoredom and adultery are the major metaphors employed by Hosea to portray the people's religious apostasy, their "running after other gods."

Hosea 1–3 perfectly illustrates this focus on Israel's apostate religious practices. Here we have a double metaphor symbolizing Israel's own infidelity to Yahweh. First, in chapters 1–2 we have the story of Hosea's marriage to Gomer and the birth of their three children: the name *Jezreel* evokes memories of the atrocities committed by King Jehu; *Lo-ruhamah* calls to mind the promise of judgment that God will have "no pity" upon Israel; and *Lo-ammi* conveys the final word of divine rejection: "You are 'not my people'; and I am not your God!" Hosea 3 changes the metaphor slightly, and no longer is the focus on a wife named Gomer and her three children who are signs of Israel's unfaithfulness. Now the focus shifts to an unnamed adulteress who is purchased by Hosea only to be sequestered away, held in solitary confinement, so to speak. She shall be cut off from all human sexual contact: she shall not be with any man (*welo' tihyi le'ish*), and Yahweh will be the same with regard to her (*wegam 'ani 'elayik*, 3:3). She shall endure a lengthy period of sexual seclusion. This threatened sequestering of the woman is a metaphor of Israel's loss of its central social infrastructure: it shall be stripped of its basic social and religious institutions, its king, prince, sacrifice, sacred pillar, ephod, and teraphim.

Hosea shows a deep indebtedness to the central religious traditions underlying the Deuteronomic theology, namely, that Israel's critical problem was its religious infidelity to Yahweh. This fascination that Israel had developed for Baal, the Canaanite god of fertility, was, in Hosea's estimation, the heart of the matter. As soon as Israel set foot in the Jordan River, as soon as the people's toes touched the fertile soil of the promised land, their appetite for larger and fuller crops, for ever-increasing wealth and security, led them to various forms of religious syncretism, worshiping the god Baal and other related deities of Canaan alongside their patron deity, Yahweh. They were unable to resist the urge of confusing Yahweh and Baal, thinking of Yahweh himself as their "owner," their "master," their "husband," their *ba'al*. Driving the theme home with repeated blows of the prophetic hammer, Hosea indicates the nature of this problem, singling out the geographical locations that called attention to Israel's most ancient corporate traditions. "Out of Egypt" God called his son, but the more God called, the further they turned away, sacrificing to the Baals and burning incense to idols (11:1-2). At Baal-peor (9:10), or at Gilgal (9:15), at Gibeah (10:9) or at Adam (6:7), over and over Hosea insists that contact with the land of promise was thoroughly contaminating.

As soon as they touched it, their relation to God turned perverse as they fell in love with the potential of grain, wine, oil, success, wealth, power, the gifts that only Yahweh as Baal, the good god of fertility, could ensure. The use of a sculpted calf as the chief symbol of the deity at the major northern sanctuaries—in Samaria, Bethel, and Dan— was particularly harshly criticized. These calves were originally not thought to represent God or Baal any more than was the ark of the covenant in Jerusalem. Indeed, Jeroboam I had instituted the bull icons as a part of a strictly Yahweh cult. By the time of Hosea, however, confusion had obviously set in, and so Hosea himself ridicules these calves as mere human inventions (8:5-6), even though people venerate them and kiss them (13:2-3). Their glory, says the prophet, shall be carted off to Assyria as tribute (10:5-6).

The Social Aspects of Israel's Offense

It *seems* as though Hosea is obsessed with the issue of religious apostasy, of worshiping the right god. It would be easy to dismiss his social critique as that of a fundamentalist religious pedant who did not care at all about issues of social justice—who cared *only* about worshiping Yahweh alone. Where is the bold social critique of Amos? Where is the concern for the poor, the orphan, the widow, the vulnerable members of society who are being crushed by the oppressive weight of the wealthy classes? Is Hosea socially irrelevant except to a few right-wing fundamentalists who want to make sure that every correct litmus test of religious purity is passed, those few who claim to know exactly who this God is that we worship, who have God confined by their precise definitions?

Before we dismiss Hosea as socially irrelevant, however, we need to consider two things. First, the metaphor of adultery is broader and more complicated than is generally acknowledged. It was not only a part of religious language, symbolizing apostasy and faithlessness. It was also a part of how one thought of political alliances with foreign countries. Allies were referred to as "lovers," and enemies as "haters." Treaty language bound the vassal country to love the lovers of the suzerain country and to hate its haters. Hosea's world was shaped by the treaties which Assyria was making with various states in western Asia, and Israel was one of the countries that flirted with Assyria in this "dance of love" (5:13), trying to secure its future in such treaty alliances (7:11). It is in this context of treaty alliances with the Assyrians that Israel is spoken of as having "hired lovers" (8:8-10). It is this bargaining with Assyria that lies behind the metaphor of Israel's "harlotry." To accuse Israel of religious infidelity was not simply a pedantic concern about correct religion. It was fundamentally a political concern about foreign alliances and the sort of pressures such alliances exerted on Israel's core religious and social values.

Second, it would be incorrect to say that Hosea was concerned only about religious matters and did not pay attention to matters of grave social concern. Hosea rehearses a long litany of social injustices, all of which result from the fact that "there is no faithfulness or kindness, and no knowledge of God in the land. There is swearing, lying, killing, stealing, and committing adultery. They break all bounds and murder follows murder" (4:1-2). Clearly, one cannot distinguish between religious and secular concerns, between matters of worshiping the correct god and worshiping God correctly. For Hosea the two go together, and offenses against God have universal and cosmic effects: "Therefore the land mourns, and all who dwell in it languish, and also the beasts of the field, and the birds of the air; and even the fish of the sea are taken away" (4:3).

Priests and the "Lack of Knowledge"

This lack of knowledge of God, according to Hosea, does not refer simply to a lack of an intellectual tradition, a shortage of professors of philosophy or theology in ancient Israel. Such knowledge was the responsibility of the priests, who were the principal "keepers of the Torah" (Jer 2:8; 18:18; Ezek 7:26). The priests were responsible for keeping Israel's story straight, for protecting that which was fundamental, constitutive, and nonnegotiable about Israel's identity. To say that the priests were simply the keepers of Torah in the sense that they were legal bureaucrats, mere clerks, is incorrect. The concept of Torah here implies the entire narrative of Israel's existence, its founding story and its charter of identity. Recall that the Hebrew word *torah* is used of the entirety of the first five books of the Hebrew Scriptures, Genesis through Deuteronomy, not just the legal materials in them.

In a bitter attack on this priestly failure to rehearse Israel's core story and identity, Hosea accuses the priests of destroying the people for this lack of knowledge (4:6). The priests, according to Hosea, were "feeding on the sin of God's people . . . greedy for their iniquity" (4:8). This is a very significant statement, though often unnoticed. In Israel, the priest was primarily responsible for altar sacrifice, including the major atoning sacrifice, the sin offering (*hatta't*). It was from the performance of such sin offerings that the priest received a part of his revenue, being rewarded with a portion of the sacrificial meat for each sacrifice (Lev 6:24—7:10). The word for "sin" and for "sin offering" is the same in Hebrew: *hatta't*. When Hosea accuses the priest of "feeding on the *sin* (*hatta't*) of the people," he is clearly referring to the well-known practice that the priest was compensated for his service by being allowed to eat a portion of the sacrifice. But if the priest were *rewarded* for remedying the people's sins, why would the priest be interested in encouraging the people to stop sinning? After all, the more the people sinned, the more the priest stood to gain. Priests were actually rewarded by encouraging the people's bad behavior, and then having the people come to the sanctuary for repentance, bringing with them more steaks and roasts. With such a system as this in place, is it likely that the community could ever be moved toward true reformation? The more altars they built in the land, the more they became altars for "sinning" (8:11). Those responsible for Israel's core identity had strongly vested interests in seeing that the system *never* changed, that the people would *always* continue on in their sin.

Hosea's Visions of Restoration

As caustic as Hosea's oracles were, they nevertheless allowed for much more hope in divine grace than did Amos's oracles. In Hosea, God is much more conflicted and unsettled than in Amos. Though the threats are clear and direct, there is also a tearing at God's heart over what to do with the people of Israel. Like a parent who is being torn apart by a rebellious child, God agonizes over what to do with Israel (6:4). Finally, recognizing that God is bound more by divine commitment to compassion and parental love than by a logical commitment to justice, God recognizes the truth of the matter: "How can I give you up, O Ephraim? How can I hand you over, O Israel? . . . My heart recoils within me, my compassion grows warm and tender. I will not execute my fierce anger, I will not again destroy Ephraim. For I am God and not mortal, the Holy One in your midst, and I will not come to destroy" (11:8-9). God's illogical compassion finally overcomes God's logical demand for justice.

Whereas Amos could only hold out a last-minute urgent plea to "seek God and live," even while the casket was being lowered into the grave, Hosea offers more vivid scenes of human repentance and divine forgiveness and reconciliation. The call to "return, O Israel, to the Lord your God" in 14:1 is accompanied by the words of genuine repentance: "Take away all guilt; accept that which is good, and we will offer the fruit of our lips. Assyria shall not save us; we will not ride upon horses; we will say no more, 'Our God,' to the work of our hands. In you the orphan finds mercy." Israel's healing is not overcome by the strength of the people themselves. If their failure had been portrayed throughout the book as a sexual addiction, it could, as an addiction, only be overcome by divine grace. "I will heal their faithlessness," says God. "I will love them freely, for my anger has turned from them. . . . They shall return and dwell beneath my shadow, they shall flourish as a garden; they shall blossom as the vine, their fragrance shall be like the wine of Lebanon" (14:4-7).

Similar words of repentance and renewal are found in 6:1-3: "Come, let us return to the Lord; for he has torn, that he may heal us; he has stricken, and he will bind us up. . . . Let us know, let us press on to know the Lord; his going forth is sure as the dawn; he will come to us as the showers, as the spring rains that water the earth." It is true that, as sincere as this repentance might be, God finds it unconvincing, since God knows that Israel's love "is like a morning cloud, like the dew that goes early away" (6:4). But these words provide a glimpse into the sort of renewal that the people can experience. Such renewal does not ultimately depend on the people's ability to overcome and master their own addiction. It is God who acts.

This intervention of God into Israel's addiction is nowhere more evident than in one of the most beautiful poetic passages in Scripture, Hosea 2:14-23. Hosea 2 presents a lengthy litany of why destruction awaits Israel. Because she has "gone after her lovers," Yahweh will *therefore* restrain her with a hedge and a wall (2:5-6). Because she did not know who it was that truly lavished upon her grain, wine, and oil, and used the silver and gold given her by Yahweh only to make idols

of Baal, Yahweh will *therefore* repossess her fortunes and cover her
with shame (2:8-13). A third *therefore* in 2:14 prepares the reader for
yet one more blow of judgment, the final and definitive blast of divine
wrath. Precisely here, however, the text takes such a strange turn
toward mercy and forgiveness that the Greek translators of the Septuagint could not believe it and so mistranslated the passage.

> Therefore, I will now allure her, and bring her into the wilderness,
> and speak tenderly to her. From there I will give her her vineyards,
> and make the Valley of Achor a door of hope. There she shall
> respond as in the days of her youth, as at the time when she came
> out of the land of Egypt. On that day, says the Lord, you will call
> me, "My husband," and no longer will you call me, "My Baal." For
> I will remove the names of the Baals from her mouth, and they shall
> be mentioned by name no more. I will make for you a covenant on
> that day with the wild animals, the birds of the air, and the creeping
> things of the ground; and I will abolish the bow, the sword, and war
> from the land; and I will make you lie down in safety. And I will
> take you for my wife forever; I will take you for my wife in righ-
> teousness and in justice, in steadfast love, and in mercy. I will take
> you for my wife in faithfulness; and you shall know the Lord. On
> that day I will answer, says the Lord, I will answer the heavens and
> they shall answer the earth; and the earth shall answer the grain,
> the wine, and the oil, and they shall answer Jezreel; and I will sow
> him for myself in the land. And I will have pity on Lo-ruhamah,
> and I will say to Lo-ammi, "You are my people"; and he shall say,
> "You are my God."

"I will allure, I will give, I will remove, I will make, I will abolish,
I will take you, I will answer, I will sow, I will have pity." It is clear
who it is that acts. Our addictions are overcome not by our own
efforts, but rather by divine initiative and outrageous grace, born out
of God's deep compassion. God is willing to forgo a commitment to
the logical iron laws of justice in order to forge a relationship based on
the illogical nature of love and compassion—a relationship in which
no longer will we call God by the title "Baal" ("owner," "master"), as
though God had to buy us and ply us with material rewards. Rather,
it will be a relationship in which we will call God "husband," a relationship marked by love and tenderness and by mutual faithfulness
one to another.

CHAPTER 4

Isaiah of Jerusalem

The Three Faces of Isaiah

It has been the long-standing opinion of scholars that the present book of Isaiah contains the oracles of several different persons who represent an "Isaiah school," coming from widely different periods of time in Israel's history. In short, chapters 1–39 are often attributed to the author referred to as "First Isaiah," chapters 40–55 to "Second Isaiah," and chapters 56–66 to "Third Isaiah." The issue is not as simple as this, however, as many of the oracles in chapters 1–39 are themselves shaped by the same spirit and hand as that which produced the oracles in chapters 40–55. Furthermore, chapters 56–66 are not as homogeneous as is the other material, and Third Isaiah is the most difficult collection to anchor in a specific historical context. In addition, given a shift in concern away from "historical" to "literary" analysis, scholarship in the last twenty years has tried to sidestep the perplexing question of the three Isaiahs entirely, and has sought instead to treat the book more holistically, regardless of the historical issues concerning its authorship. For my purposes, however, I will maintain the distinction, as it is helpful in placing the oracles of the different authors in a particular context.

First Isaiah is often referred to as Isaiah of Jerusalem, given his close connection to the Jerusalem tradition and ideology as well as the temple complex itself. It is this Isaiah who also appears extensively in the Deuteronomistic History (especially 2 Kings 19–20). Isaiah of Jerusalem lived during the reigns of the Judean kings Uzziah, Jotham, Ahaz, and Hezekiah, and was approximately contemporary with the prophets Amos and Hosea. The prophet known as Second Isaiah, however, is generally considered to have lived during the period of the Babylonian exile; he looks forward to the imminent victory of the Persian king Cyrus, whom he so highly regards as part of the divine plan for Judah's restoration that he gives Cyrus the title "Messiah" ("anointed one," Isa 45:1; cf. 44:28; 45:13). In addition to this direct reference to Cyrus, the language calling for the captive Judeans to prepare for their restoration to the land of Israel gives scholars confidence that Second Isaiah lived just prior to Cyrus's victory over the Babylonians and the promulgation of his edict permitting the return of the Jews in 539 B.C.E.—in other words, approximately two hundred years after Isaiah of Jerusalem began his ministry.

Third Isaiah, though more difficult to locate in a specific historical context, is generally thought to have conducted his prophetic ministry in this Isaianic tradition during the years following the restoration. The mood of these chapters is considerably more somber and troubled, depicting not the flush of optimism characteristic of Second Isaiah but rather witnessing to the problems and frustrations that plagued the people of Judah in trying to restore their culture and society some generations later. Confronted by opposition from within and without (cf. the books of Ezra and Nehemiah) as well as by a corporate lethargy that crippled the initial attempts at reconstruction, Third Isaiah has to reevaluate what it means to be Israel and demonstrates the struggles for identity that confronted the people in these difficult years.

All three voices, however, bear witness to a common prophetic tradition, and it is important to read the book in its entirety in order to hear the collective voice of Isaiah.

The Beginning of Isaiah's Prophetic Ministry

The most certain date we have to judge when Isaiah first began his ministry is that provided in 6:1, dating Isaiah's temple vision to the "year that King Uzziah died." Uzziah's death is commonly dated to

742 B.C.E., and therefore many scholars, taking Isaiah 6 to be a rehearsal of Isaiah's call narrative, assume that Isaiah began his ministry in that year. It seems to me, however, that Isaiah 6 is not a call narrative but rather has a different function, similar to the function provided by 1 Kings 22 in relation to the ministry of the prophet Micaiah ben Imlah. Both stories—Isaiah 6 and 1 Kings 22—recall a visionary experience that the prophet has of the divine presence. But 1 Kings 22 is certainly not Micaiah's call narrative, as the text itself indicates that Micaiah had long been a member of the royal prophetic corps. Similar to 1 Kings 22, Isaiah 6 attempts to explain the dynamic at work in Isaiah's *ongoing* prophetic ministry.

In Isaiah 6 the prophet has a vision of the divine presence in which God solicits a volunteer to carry a message to Judah. Without flinching and without having a clue as to what this message is, Isaiah eagerly volunteers: "Here am I; send me!" But then comes the awful message that Isaiah is instructed to carry: "Make the mind of this people dull, and stop their ears, and shut their eyes, so that they may not look with their eyes, and listen with their ears, and comprehend with their minds, and turn and be healed." Given this awful task of insuring judgment, Isaiah can only ask in horrified disbelief, "How long, O Lord?" The answer comes: "Until cities lie waste without inhabitant, and houses without people, and the land is utterly desolate; until the Lord sends everyone far away, and vast is the emptiness in the midst of the land."

There is no indication that this is the *beginning* of Isaiah's ministry. Indeed, I believe that chapters 1–5 have been placed where they are because the editor of the material wanted the reader to know that they come *before* the scene reported in chapter 6, and that chapter 6 is a response to these earlier chapters. If Isaiah 6 is dated to the year of King Uzziah's death (742 B.C.E.), then chapters 1–5 must be the oracles thought to have been delivered by Isaiah prior to Uzziah's death. If they come from approximately the years 745 to 742, we can easily regard Isaiah as roughly a contemporary of both Amos and Hosea. Whereas their ministries were to the north, to the nation of Israel, Isaiah's ministry was to the south, to Judah and to the royal and religious establishment in Jerusalem.

When considering the ministries of Amos and Hosea, we saw how their word was addressed in large measure to the social ills created by the wealth and power of the period of Jeroboam II in the north. Uzziah of Judah was the southern equivalent of Jeroboam, and his kingdom too had enjoyed the same sort of international conditions enjoyed by the north. The temporary Assyrian weakness allowed Judah also to participate in increased trade and military expansionism, leading to growing wealth and power enjoyed by the few at the expense of the masses of increasingly oppressed poor. It is no surprise whatsoever, then, that these early oracles of Isaiah in chapters 1–5 sound like they could have been cloned from the oracles of Amos himself.

These chapters focus upon the prophet's warnings issued in 1:14-17:

> Your new moons and your appointed festivals my soul hates; they have become a burden to me, I am weary of bearing them. When you stretch out your hands, I will hide my eyes from you; even though you make many prayers, I will not listen; your hands are full of blood. Wash yourselves; make yourselves clean; remove the evil of your doings from before my eyes; cease to do evil, learn to do good; seek justice, rescue the oppressed, defend the orphan, plead for the widow.

The central message, so similar to that of the prophet Amos, is sounded in the biting and satirical song about the Lord's vineyard in 5:1-7. In spite of God's tender care, the vineyard did not yield "justice" (*mishpat*) but rather "bloodshed" (*mispah*). God had expected "righteousness" (*tsedaqah*), but instead he heard only a "cry of desperation" (*tse'aqah*). In this light, chapter 6, the vision in which Isaiah is told to harden their hearts, to "stop their ears," and to "shut their eyes," is read as God's response to the failure of Isaiah's initial ministry. The powerful Amos-like punch of Isaiah's opening oracles in chapters 1–5 was to no avail, and so the judgment was ensured. Isaiah then drops out of public sight in the year 742 B.C.E., embarking on a lengthy hiatus in his ministry. One might wonder if a sense of failure led to a need to regather his courage.

Isaiah and the Syro-Ephraimite Crisis

The next we hear of Isaiah is about eight years later, during a crisis known as the Syro-Ephraimite war against Judah. By this time Assyria to the east had again overcome its temporary difficulties and turned once more to establish control over the western Asian nations in order to ensure access to the Mediterranean Sea. Afraid of being conquered by the giant and aggressive Assyrians, these western nations, as in the past, formed a coalition in an attempt to hold off the Assyrians. The countries of Aram (Syria) and Israel formed an alliance, and wanted Judah to be the third partner with them. But the king of Judah, who by this time was King Ahaz, dragged his feet at the invitation. For one reason or another, he decided not to join them in their coalition. This so angered the coalition forces of Israel and Aram that they invaded Judah in order to force Ahaz to join. This invasion and war took place from 734 to 732 B.C.E., and is the context for the material we read in Isaiah 7–8.

The primary perspective of Isaiah, now faced with a regenerated Assyrian power and a radical reconfiguration of international politics, changed to address the situation at hand. His message was now shaped by the international intrigue in which Judah and King Ahaz were caught up. Isaiah's message was no longer directly related to the same set of problems as those addressed some eight years earlier, shaped by the social corruption of the wealthy and fat years under Uzziah. His message now related to what Judah should do in the face of international disaster: trust in God. Do not trust in foreign alliances; do not trust in your own strength and military prowess. Do not look to your strong neighbors for support, whether Egypt or Assyria itself. God will take care of these two invading kings of Israel and Aram, these two "smoldering stumps of firebrands." Trust in God. If you do not trust you will never be able to stand.

The Sign of Immanuel as a "Prophecy" of Salvation

In this context, Isaiah enlists the support of his sons in order to make his point: Shear-jashub ("a remnant shall return") and Maher-shalal-hash-baz ("fast is the booty, speedy the prey"). They confront King Ahaz with the promise that if he will trust in God's power to deliver, the invasion of the Israel-Aram coalition will fail (7:1-9; 8:1-4). In this same context we then hear of another prophecy focusing on the name of a child who will be called Immanuel, "God is with us." Of course, this story has become famous in Christian tradition as the primary prophecy of Jesus, to be born of the virgin Mary. It is taken as a prophecy relating directly to this child, born of a virgin according to the words of Isaiah (Matt 1:23).

The idea of Jesus' divine conception, born of the virgin Mary, has come to play an important role in the theology of the church, and certainly conveys the truth that *this* child, God incarnate, the Word made flesh, is like no other child in human history. That truth is central to the proclamation of the church and cannot be compromised. It is, however, only fair and judicious if we consider the words of this prophecy in their original context within the words spoken by Isaiah himself. Three points must be made.

First, the vocabulary of the passage must be given special consideration. The Hebrew text clearly indicates that the woman in question is an *'almah*, that is, a "young woman" who has reached puberty and is now socially available for marriage. This is not the Hebrew word for "virgin," which is *betulah*. Further, this *'almah* is not simply *any* young woman but is rather *the* young woman, as though Isaiah is pointing to someone walking by or to someone well known to King Ahaz. Further, this young woman is not going to become pregnant at some future time, but she is *already* pregnant, and she is, as Isaiah speaks, in the process of bearing this child. The Hebrew verbs are clear on this matter: "she *has become* pregnant" (*harah*, a verb in the past tense) and "she is *presently* bearing this child" (*weyoledet*, a participle, indicating immediacy).

Second, one must consider the formal question of what a prophecy is in relation to a sign (*'ot*). Consider the case of 1 Kings 13, which relates the strange confrontation of a prophetic figure with King Jeroboam I of Israel. The word of the prophecy, relating to the distant event of the appearance of King Josiah nearly three hundred years later, is followed by the giving of a sign, which takes place immediately (1 Kgs 13:1-3). This story, as strange and as fabricated as it is, nevertheless perfectly illustrates how a sign relates to a prophetic oracle. The sign is seen as the immediate down payment on the more distantly envisioned fulfillment of the prophecy. The prophecy speaks to events further off. The sign is immediately at hand, serving to give evidence of the veracity and power as well as the effectiveness of the prophetic word. Note that in Isaiah 7, it is not a prophecy that Isaiah offers King Ahaz. Rather, it is a sign. Isaiah turns to Ahaz and, drawing Ahaz's attention to someone in mind, says that the birth of her child is a sign. The so-called Immanuel prophecy is, form critically, not a prophecy at all. It is intended to be the immediate down payment on the truth of a prophetic word.

Third, one must place the significance of this sign of Immanuel within the context of the prophecy to which it relates. The prophetic word proper is Isaiah's message about the Syro-Ephraimite crisis, given in verse 16: "For before the child knows how to refuse the evil and choose the good, the land before whose two kings you are in dread will be deserted." That is the prophetic word, relating to the defeat of the kings of Israel and Aram. The "Immanuel sign" takes its meaning from that larger promise—the promise that, if Ahaz will but trust in God, trust that God is in fact "with us" (*'immanu'el*), then the prophetic word will come to pass. God will indeed deliver Judah from its enemies.

The words of this sign were transformed in later tradition to function as a prophecy, and it became very important for some in the early church. It was, for example, important for Matthew's telling of the birth story, and Matthew refers to Isaiah 7 when telling of the promise of a child to be born to this virgin, whose name would be Immanuel (Matt 1:23). But it was not important to either Mark or John, who do not refer to it at all, preferring to move in other directions to tell their respective stories. The prophecy may not have even been important for Luke, in whose telling the child is referred to as "the son of the Most High" (Luke 1:32), there being no reference at all to the name Immanuel or to the Isaianic prophecy. Nor was it important to Paul in any of his writings or theological reflection. Indeed, when Paul thinks about the physical aspects of the birth of Jesus (Gal 4:4), he stresses not the special nature of the birth but rather its human and common (or fleshly) aspects: "But when the fullness of time had come, God sent his Son, *born of a woman, born under the law*, in order to redeem those who were under the law, so that we might receive adoption as children." One wonders if Paul or any other writer was aware of the tradition of the virginal conception of Jesus as fulfillment of prophecy. If they were, it certainly did not play even a minor role in their view of who this Jesus was.

The underlying truth of what later became a doctrine and, more unfortunately, a test of one's orthodoxy, cannot be compromised. This child, God incarnate, the divine emptied of all pretensions and taking human form, even that of the death on a cross, is like no other child. To understand this child in the terms of Isaiah's words to Ahaz is but one attempt to understand how God is at work in Jesus, how God is fully involved with the human condition. However, we ought not so stress the importance of the language of Isaiah 7 that we lose sight of the overwhelming importance of the truth that God is at work in Christ. Nor ought we hurry from Isaiah's sign that he gave to Ahaz to overlook the words of the prophecy: if we will but *trust*, God will provide the deliverance.

Assyria as the "Rod of Yahweh's Anger"

Throughout this period, Isaiah came to an increasing understanding that God was not just at work in young women and in babies named Immanuel. God was also at work in the fearful and momentous events of international history. God was even at work in the Assyrians. We shall see in the next chapter how Isaiah's view of the Assyrians came to be fully developed. At this early stage of his ministry, during the years 734–732 B.C.E., the view was still blurred and foggy. Isaiah understood that God would deliver Judah by the hand of the Assyrians, that it was they who would rescue Judah from the onslaught of the Israelite/Aramaean coalition (8:4-7). But Isaiah also knew that such deliverance was a two-edged sword and that, once unsheathed, this sword would also be lethal for Judah. Assyria would be a "razor" in the hand of God used to shave Judah down to the bone, to shave every fiber of body hair that the people had (7:20). The Assyrians would be, according to Isaiah, the "rod of Yahweh's anger" turned loose on Judah (8:7-8; 10:5-6).

How ironic it was, then, that King Ahaz turned precisely to Assyria itself for relief (2 Kgs 16:7-9). Instead of trusting in God, the central message of Isaiah of Jerusalem, King Ahaz offered himself and his nation to the Assyrians as a vassal state, and took on all the cultural and religious obligations incumbent on a vassal. The "rod of Yahweh's anger" would soon become the oppressive power against which God's word would be directed. But for that chapter we must wait. Following the Syro-Ephraimite crisis and Ahaz's decision to trust in Assyria rather than in God, Isaiah once again left the battlefield, undoubtedly in frustration and defeat. This time his hiatus would not last a mere eight years as before. We would not see Isaiah again for nearly thirty years, by which time history would once again take a dramatic turn.

CHAPTER 5

Isaiah and the Assyrian Crisis

Out of Retirement

Isaiah of Jerusalem burst onto the prophetic stage with hammerlike oracles during the reign of Uzziah of Judah. These oracles, similar to those of Amos, focused on the social abuses of Judah's leaders and the injustices perpetrated against the poor and oppressed. But with Uzziah's death in 742 B.C.E. Isaiah left the field, unable to crack the concrete facade of Judah's social indifference, only able to sense that he had, in some way, hardened their hearts, stuffed their ears, closed their eyes, and ensured their judgment. Eight years later Isaiah was back, this time trying to convince King Ahaz that he should trust only in God's power to deliver and refrain from making any "alliances with death" in the face the Syro-Ephraimite war. But once again his ministry met with failure, as Ahaz opted for the Assyrians rather than God. In this year, 732 B.C.E., Isaiah once again took his leave from public ministry.

It was only thirty years later that Isaiah clearly reemerged in his public ministry. Though he must have been an elderly statesman by this time, one wonders if he might not have been prompted out of "retirement" and back into public view by the widening political and social crisis, a crisis he could not resist addressing. The Assyrians were back, hammering away in one military campaign after another, year after year. This time they were at the very doors of Jerusalem. Now it was King Hezekiah who was on the throne, the last of a long line of monarchs under whom Isaiah exercised his ministry. If in his earlier days Isaiah had understood that the Assyrians had something to do with God's plan for Judah, that they were the "rod of Yahweh's anger," it all had by now become clear what that role was. The Assyrians were threatening to devour Judah. Having already besieged and conquered all of the military fortifications of Judah, such as that at Lachish to the southwest, they were now laying siege to Jerusalem itself.

A number of oracles in the book of Isaiah point to the shifting attitude Isaiah took toward the Assyrians during these circumstances: if they were indeed the "rod of Yahweh's anger," then they would in turn be punished for their violent excess. If God had intended them only to implement divine judgment on Israel and Aram, the Assyrians had other plans—world domination. But God would, when finished using Assyria to accomplish the divine plan, turn on Assyria itself and punish it for its arrogant boasting and its imperial and pretentious pride (Isa 10:7-12). If the ax would vaunt itself over the one who wields it, then God would in turn fashion an ax of his own against the Assyrians (10:15-16).

Isaiah's Intercession for Jerusalem

One of the interesting facts of the phenomenon of prophecy in Israel is that, as I mentioned before, none of the prophets whom we know from their written oracles figures significantly in the Deuteronomistic History (Joshua through 2 Kings) other than Isaiah. Jonah is referred to in a minor way in 2 Kings 14:25, but his mention there is incidental. When we meet Isaiah there, it is precisely this late Isaiah whom we meet—the older statesman, called out of retirement to take up the challenge one more time. One might wonder why the younger Isaiah never appears in the historical narrative in 2 Kings. It may be because the message of the early Isaiah did not lend itself nearly as well to the strategy of the historian as did the more salvific message of the later Isaiah.

According to 2 Kings 18–20, on four different occasions Isaiah gives a prophetic oracle to King Hezekiah, and two of these involve promises of deliverance from the Assyrians. In 2 Kings 19:1-7 Isaiah is consulted by a desperate Hezekiah, who has just been given a crippling message by the Assyrians: surrender or face destruction! Isaiah's message is direct and to the point: God will put a spirit in the king of Assyria, and he will hear a rumor causing him to return to Assyria, where he will be killed. The second episode, in 2 Kings 19:14-34, is an expanded version of this same event. Again Hezekiah comes with a threatening letter that he has received from the Assyrians and prays in the temple before God, asking for divine deliverance. Again Isaiah responds with a salvific oracle, once more predicting an Assyrian retreat (vv. 28, 32-34).

What is peculiar about this text is that it is followed by the curious story concerning the "angel of Yahweh" who overcame the Assyrian camp outside Jerusalem at night and slaughtered 185,000 Assyrian warriors, leaving their dead bodies on the ground in the morning. This narrative addition to the plot certainly goes beyond anything suggested by the oracles themselves, which speak only of an Assyrian retreat. It is generally believed to be a legendary embroidering of the basic story of the Assyrians retreating from Jerusalem for other unknown reasons (a rumor of rebellion at home, perhaps, or a need to redirect the army against Egypt). I think it likely that the story of the angelic massacre found its way into the story under the influence of Isaiah 10:16-18 and 24-27. Those texts speak, in figurative and symbolic language, of God afflicting the Assyrians with "wasting sickness" (*razon*, literally "leanness, wasting away") and a "whip . . . as when he struck Midian at the rock of Oreb." The event at the rock of Oreb did not involve any plague, but rather refers to the confusion into which the Midianite army was thrown as a result of the surprise attack at night led by Gideon (Judg 7:19-25). These figurative references in Isaiah to a surprise attack at night connected to the note of Assyrian troops being struck by "wasting away" was taken up by the historian who embellished the account of the destruction of the Assyrian troops by relating that they were decimated by an angelic attack that obliterated the entire Assyrian army in one night.

There are actually three different accounts of Isaiah's ministry to King Hezekiah in the context of this final Assyrian crisis and siege of Jerusalem. The account of the Deuteronomistic History in 2 Kings 18–20 is taken over in great detail by the final editor of the book of Isaiah, where the account is reported in Isaiah 37–39. The only major difference between the accounts in 2 Kings and Isaiah is that Isaiah 38:9-20 adds the words of the prayer of thanksgiving spoken by Hezekiah upon his being healed by Isaiah. Otherwise these two accounts are quite close in detail. The surprise is how the Chronicler handles this material in relating the events as part of the retelling of Israel's history in 2 Chronicles 32. Basically, the Chronicler abbreviates these stories to a summary statement and writes Isaiah out of the story. In all four of the episodes, Isaiah is mentioned only in the second, and even there he simply prays alongside King Hezekiah for deliverance (2 Chr 32:20), never giving any oracle at all. In all probability, the Chronicler wanted to stress the importance of Hezekiah, whose wonderful deeds of cultic restoration the Chronicler rehearsed in considerable detail (2 Chr 29:3—31:21). In order to enhance Hezekiah's prestige, the Chronicler minimized the involvement of Isaiah in each of these episodes.

Isaiah's Visions of Restoration

We know nothing of Isaiah's family background or social status, only that he was "the son of Amoz" (Isa 1:1). There is no indication that he was a priest or royal official. Unlike Jeremiah and Ezekiel, both of whom, the reader is told, were from priestly families (Jer 1:1; Ezek 1:3), there is no such hint regarding Isaiah. What is clear, however, is that Isaiah was closely connected to the temple establishment in Jerusalem. In the texts from 2 Kings considered above, Hezekiah went to the temple to pray on both occasions when the divine word was sought (2 Kgs 19:1, 14). Neither text necessitates Isaiah's presence there, as both passages suggest that word was sent to the prophet. But Hezekiah would not have had to go to the temple to pray (compare 2 Kgs 20:1-11, where it is apparently Isaiah who makes a "house call" on Hezekiah). That Hezekiah went to the temple and that word was sent to Isaiah at least suggest the possibility that Isaiah was associated with the temple precinct in these situations. Furthermore, the vision that Isaiah reported in Isaiah 6:1-7 certainly indicates a familiarity not only with the temple in general but with the inner sanctum and its vocabulary and iconography. This iconography included the ark of the covenant, thought of as Yahweh's throne, along with the presence of seraphim, probably stylized winged serpents associated with the cult of Yahweh until the days of Hezekiah (cf. Num 21:6-8; Isa 14:29;

and 30:6; on Hezekiah's reform, during which the Nehushtan pole was removed from the temple, cf. 2 Kgs 18:4). If Isaiah was not a priest, he was at least a member of the royal prophetic corps that surrounded Hezekiah as a part of the royal palace/temple complex.

This close association of Isaiah with Jerusalem was certainly evident in Isaiah's oracles, as we saw above. The Assyrians, he stated, would never be able to enter the city of Jerusalem, nor even to fire an arrow into the city. "For I will defend this city to save it," says God, "for my own sake and for the sake of my servant David" (2 Kgs 19:32-34). Some of the most beautiful oracles of Isaiah focus on this attachment to the city of Jerusalem and to God's purposes for its protection and restoration. Isaiah's deep commitment to the throne of David and the government of peace and justice that flows from it was central to his identity. As in his earlier ministry, when a child to be named Immanuel was a sign of God's promise of deliverance if the king would but trust, so now another child comes to the fore. A child would be born upon whose shoulders the government of Jerusalem would be placed. "Wonderful Counselor, Mighty God, Everlasting Father, Prince of Peace"—the royal titles for the king who would carry Isaiah's increasingly messianic hopes.

Isaiah's commitment to the messianic promises associated with the Davidic monarchy is also seen in the often rehearsed text of Isaiah 11:1-5, the shoot that will sprout forth from the stump of Jesse. Jesse, the father of David, the root system of Judah's national aspirations, is the symbol for Judah's future hopes. The spirit of Yahweh will rest upon him: wisdom, understanding, counsel, might, knowledge, and fear of God. His rule will ensure justice and equity, with care for the poor and humble. Such hopes for the specific city of Jerusalem then give way to universal visions of cosmic solidarity: the wolf shall live with the lamb, and the leopard shall sleep with young goats; calves and lions, all led by a little child. Not just Jerusalem, but the entire *earth*, "will be full of the knowledge of Yahweh as the waters covering the sea" (Isa 11:6-9).

Confidence and Trust in God

All through Isaiah's prophetic ministry, the core of his message was a call to trust in the God of the promise to David. Most pointedly stated in his middle years to King Ahaz when faced with his own crisis of state, Isaiah's words were direct: "If you will not trust you will not be entrusted" (*'im lo' ta'aminu ki lo' te'amenu*, Isa 7:9). But such trust is difficult to muster, particularly when confronted with the crises such as those faced by Kings Ahaz and Hezekiah. As we saw, Ahaz capitulated to the logic of international politics and sought deliverance from the invading armies of Israel and Aram by linking Judah's fortunes to those of the Assyrians. Ahaz invited the Assyrians to become the overlords of Judah, and in making this covenant with death, Ahaz also committed Judah to pay tribute to Assyrian deities and to the treasuries of Nineveh and Calah. Ahaz found it impossible to rely on anything other than the logical assurance of politics as usual. Paying tribute to Assyria, even visiting the Assyrian King in Damascus and seeing the splendors of the way the Assyrians worshiped their gods, led Ahaz to update the architecture of the Jerusalem temple itself (2 Kgs 16:10-18). Such an act was certainly no benign remodeling to make a simple fashion statement. It was an action of subservience, of acquiescence to Assyrian domination. Symbolizing Ahaz's capitulation to political necessity and Assyrian control, it represented the extent to which Ahaz could find trust only in his newfound friends from Assyria.

Unlike Ahaz, however, his son Hezekiah "did what was right in the sight of Yahweh," according to the words of the Deuteronomistic Historian (2 Kgs 18:3). He is one of just a very few kings to have scored such high ratings in the estimation of this tough critic. His achievements are summarized in 2 Kings 18:5: "He trusted in Yahweh." The historian was so impressed with Hezekiah that he gave him stellar marks: "There was none like him among all the kings of Judah after him, or among those who were before him." One might think, then, that Hezekiah would be a model of what it meant to adhere to Isaiah's call to trust.

But what does such trust entail? Does it mean to stand by passively in the face of danger and refuse to engage the hard political realities of life, waiting idly for God to act? If Hezekiah is a model of such trust, it is not because of his passivity. Few kings were more active than was Hezekiah in trying to secure the safety of Jerusalem. There is a cryptic reference in the Deuteronomistic History to the fact that Hezekiah "made the pool and the conduit and brought water into the city" (2 Kgs 20:20). This easily missed historical note is telling for what such trust entails. If one compares this note to the Chronicler's History, there we find a fuller explanation of what it was that Hezekiah did.

Soon after it became apparent that the Assyrians were about to lay siege to Jerusalem, Hezekiah initiated a massive engineering project to tunnel through the mountain on which Jerusalem was built in order to bring water from its source at the Gihon Spring into a major reservoir inside the city walls, so that the city's water supply could be ensured and the Assyrian army deprived of easy access to water (2 Chr 32:2-4). But Hezekiah also apparently refortified Jerusalem with new walls and defensive towers and initiated a massive weapons production campaign (32:5-8). Though Hezekiah's rhetoric stressed the "divine" nature of Israel's defenses (v. 8), Hezekiah was not passively deferring to a naïve trust that God would somehow handle it all.

The Problems That Trust Brings

Trust in God, but make sure that your walls are solid, your weapons stockpiled, and your water secure! Such trust, we might think, is only marginally different from that exercised by Ahaz in his trust in the armies of Assyria. The point, however, is that trust is not naïve. Trust is not the adoption of unrealistic hope in divine intervention that leads to human inaction and passivity. Trust brings with it a willingness to enter the fray and to participate as an active agent in securing one's own vision of the future. One might even dare to say that the reign of God is too important to be left to God alone. We need to steer between the dangerous rocks of Scylla and Charybdis, between the illusion that we have any control over our ultimate destiny and the equally dangerous assumption that we have none. We must understand ourselves to be active agents at work with God in living life faithfully. We must trust that our lives of faith, our commitments to justice and fairness, and our witness to God's vision of peace for the entire cosmos do make a difference. Such commitments to justice, to fairness, to peace and the cosmic vision of restoration envisioned by Isaiah—those are our walls, our weapons, and our sources of water. They do not have a voice in the world if we passively stand aside and trust that God will be interested in pursuing the divine will without our active engagement.

Such trust can easily be turned inside out, however, so that it becomes not only a naïve commitment to passivity but also a naïve assumption of divine grace. Isaiah's message was that, if the king would but trust, God would be with the people to deliver them—

Immanuel, "God is with us." Many suggest, however, that Isaiah was walking a thin line when promising that Jerusalem was inviolable to Assyrian arrows and siege ramps. The ideology of Jerusalem's inviolability may go back to its very origins and have been a part of its own mythos, its own delusional self-perception. Recall the words of the Jebusites as they stood on the walls of Jerusalem shouting down at David and his troops: "You will not come in here, even the blind and the lame will turn you back" (2 Sam 5:6). It could be argued that the worst thing to happen to Jerusalem was that Isaiah's prophecy that the Assyrian siege of Jerusalem would fail came true. Jerusalem was spared. As the legend of the angelic massacre of the Assyrian troops developed and became part of the historical narrative, the situation became worse. One hundred years later Jeremiah stood in the temple courts faced with the popular sentiment that God would ensure the safety of this place simply because it was "the temple of Yahweh." "Do not trust in these deceptive words: 'This is the temple of the Lord, the temple of the Lord, the temple of the Lord,'" says Jeremiah (Jer 7:1-15). Is it possible that Jeremiah, some one hundred years after Isaiah, would face a problem created by the end result of Isaiah's prophecy? Trusting in the automatic goodness and generosity, the profligate grace of God turns Isaiah's word on its head.

In spite of these dangerous excesses, Isaiah has left us some of the most sublime prophetic words in Scripture—visions of wolves and lambs, of lions and kid goats, of little children playing with snakes, of universal restoration and peace, and of the messianic promise of one whose governing would be upheld "with justice and with righteousness from this time onward and for evermore. The zeal of Yahweh of hosts will do this" (9:7).

CHAPTER 6

Micah of Moresheth

Micah in the Memory of the Community

The prophet Micah is known in Christian circles primarily for two of his prophecies. One is the prophecy in 5:2 concerning Bethlehem of Ephrathah, "who are too little even to be among the clans of Judah; from you shall come forth for me one who is to be ruler in Israel." This oracle is cited in Matthew 2:6 as the text to which the chief priests and scribes referred when telling Herod where it was that the Messiah was to be born. It has become an essential part of our Christmas pageants, but its popularity is chiefly limited to that context. The other oracle for which Micah is remembered is 6:6-8, which is one of the clearest and boldest statements in the Bible relating forms of religious practice to the basic commitments of social justice:

> "With what shall I come before the Lord, and bow myself before God on high? Shall I come before him with burnt offerings, with calves a year old? Will the Lord be pleased with thousands of rams, with ten thousands of rivers of oil? Shall I give my firstborn for my transgression, the fruit of my body for the sin of my soul?" He has showed you, O mortal, what is good; and what does the Lord require of you but to do justice, and to love kindness, and to walk humbly with your God?

That Micah should be remembered for such oracles is interesting, because it probably shows how a prophet's words are always placed in a context that filters the way we hear the prophet. The story of Jesus' birth in Bethlehem of Ephrathah and the modern liberal commitments to social justice are the filters through which we have sifted Micah to extract from it what little anyone recalls. But what is interesting is that these texts in Micah are not at all what was memorable about the prophet in the period soon after his death.

Micah is the one prophet who gives us a look at what one might call "inner-canonical interpretation." Some literary themes and allusions were carried over from one prophetic book to another, but never does any writing prophet quote another writing prophet by name. One wonders if they ever read the collections of oracles attributed to their earlier colleagues. The one exception is Micah. Micah, whose prophetic ministry was exercised in the last quarter of the eighth century B.C.E. (ca. 725–700 B.C.E.), is the only prophet whose oracles were directly cited in a later prophetic book. In Jeremiah 26, in a scene that takes place in about 609 B.C.E. (in other words, about a hundred years after Micah lived), we find an interesting situation in which Jeremiah is being tried before a jury of royal and temple officials. The officials are debating what action should be taken to stop Jeremiah. In this context, the elders of the people think back to the hundred-year-old case of Micah and cite it as a precedent to help them think through this matter of what they should do with Jeremiah. When they think back to Micah they do not remember the oracle about Bethlehem of Ephrathah and the coming "ruler of Israel." Nor do they recall the oracle about what it is that God requires: "justice, love, and humility." What they recall is the final words of judgment in Micah 3:12: "Zion shall be plowed as a field; Jerusalem shall become a heap of ruins and the mountain of the house a wooded height" (Jer 26:18).

The fact that, one hundred years later, Micah is remembered precisely for these words is interesting for two reasons: first for what it tells us about the editing of the book of Micah, and second for what it tells us about how the prophet understood his task. According to Micah's own words (3:8), he understood his prophetic task as "declaring to Jacob his transgression and to Israel his sin." This focus on judgment is characteristic of chapters 1–3, and is certainly the point of that oracle recalled in the days of Jeremiah. But it is not characteristic of much of the rest of the book. A much more salvific viewpoint and curious anachronistic references, such as that to Babylon in 4:10, suggest that much of the material in chapters 4–7 comes from a different and later hand. In this case, when quoting Micah 3:12, the elders in Jeremiah 26 may have been citing what they would have known as the conclusion to the earliest oracles comprising the collection of the prophecy of Micah, that is, what we now have as chapters 1–3.

But the curious reference to Micah found in Jeremiah 26 is also interesting for what it tells us about prophetic ministry. Micah's word was that "Zion shall be plowed as a field; Jerusalem shall become a heap of ruins, and the mountain of the house a wooded height." But this did not come to pass during the days of Hezekiah, when these words were spoken. People would surely have wondered about why Micah's words did not come true. There would have been only a few possible ways of interpreting this noneffectiveness of the prophetic word. Some may have argued that Micah was simply a failure who prophesied a failed word. He was, quite simply, wrong. Enough of these sorts of prophetic misses would have had Micah thrown into the group known as "lying prophets." On the other hand, others may have argued that Micah's word simply had not come true—yet! But give it time and it would. Micah was just ahead of his time, and his word needed a generation or two, or five, in order to reach its conclusion and fulfillment.

So Micah could have been recalled either as a failed prophet or as a prophet ahead of his time, so good that he could see into even the *distant* future, the future, dare one say, of Jesus of Nazareth. Note, however, that neither of these options is how the people understood Micah's prophecy during the days of Jeremiah. They regarded Micah neither as a failed prophet because his oracle was never fulfilled, nor as a success far beyond normal capabilities because his oracle was not *yet* fulfilled. Rather, they considered Micah's oracle and ministry to have been successful, but for a far different reason: because it prompted King Hezekiah to repent. With Hezekiah's repentance came God's own repentance, so God did not have to carry through the threat that had been articulated in Micah's oracle of judgment (Jer 26:19). God remains unbound even by the prophetic word, free to change the course even of the divinely spoken word. The greatest success a prophet can have is not the success of a fulfilled prediction, but rather the repentance of the people and the renewal of their relationship with God.

Micah's Background and Prophetic Identity

Micah was from Moresheth-gath, a small town in the foothills south-west of Jerusalem (1:14; Jer 26:18). Moresheth was not simply a pastoral village, but probably also was a military and administrative outpost of Jerusalem, part of the rings of the defense network of Judah, and perhaps a royal storehouse and armory. Micah's roots in rural Judah account for his perspective, which differs considerably from that of the urban Isaiah. Whereas Isaiah revered Jerusalem and considered it to be of special importance to God's divine plan, inviolable to the enemy and specially blessed by messianic promises, Micah understood Jerusalem to be nothing less than "the high place of Judah," the southern equivalent to Samaria, the "transgression of Jacob" in the north (1:5).

The book of Micah does not reveal much to us about how Micah understood his position and his role within the larger social structures of Judah and the royal/temple establishment. The superscription to the book (Mic 1:1) refers to Micah as having *seen* the word of Yahweh, using the verb *hazah*, from which the term *hozeh* or "visionary" is derived. But it is difficult to tell whether Micah would have referred to himself as a *hozeh*, or even what it would have meant had he done so. Recall that the book of Amos begins with the same attribution, talking about the "words . . . which he *saw* (*hazah*)." Yet when Amos is called a "visionary" or *hozeh* by the priest Amaziah in Amos 7:12, Amos refuses the term, saying, "I am not a *prophet* (*nabi'*)." Were the terms *nabi'* and *hozeh* interchangeable by the time of Amos and Micah? Were either of the terms meant with a derisive and derogatory meaning, as if to refer to the prophet as a lunatic? Superscriptions were added to prophetic books at such a later date and from such a different editorial perspective that they probably cannot be used to give any sense of how the prophet would have understood himself.

In Micah 3:5-8 Micah attacks the prophets "who, when biting with their teeth, declare 'Peace,' but if a person does not put anything into their mouths, they sanctify war against him." Prophets (*nebi'im*), seers (*hozim*), and diviners (*qosemim*) shall all be disgraced and shamed. Then Micah goes on to say, "But as for me, I am filled with power, with the spirit of the Lord, and with justice and might, to declare to Jacob his transgression and to Israel his sin" (3:6-8). The question here is whether Micah sees himself as standing over against *all* of the prophets, or whether he sees himself as standing *among* them, and criticizing them from within their ranks. Do his words "As for me" indicate that he understood himself to be a *true* prophet, or do they indicate that he *hated* prophets and wanted to distance himself from them? Would Micah himself have wanted to be identified as "among the prophets"? Or would he, as Amos apparently did, reject the label, echoing Amos's words: "I am not a prophet nor a member of a prophetic group"? It is impossible to tell how Micah thought of himself in relationship to the larger category of prophets.

Another interesting text is Micah 2:6-11, where Micah reflects on the reception that he has received from those who have heard his words. "'Do not *preach*'—thus they preach—'one should not preach of such things.'" Micah concludes by saying, "If someone were to go about uttering empty falsehoods, saying, 'I will preach to you of wine and strong drink,' such a one would be the preacher for this people!" The verb used here ("preach" [*nataf*]) seems to be a technical term for what it is that prophets do (so also in Amos 7:16; Ezek 21:2). But the primary meaning of the word has to do with what liquids do: they "pour out," or "drip." The verb *nataf* can be associated with rain or dew dripping from the sky (Judg 5:4; Ps 68:8-9; Job 29:22), but it is more frequently associated with substances that are sweet, sticky, or fragrant, such as honey, myrrh, and wine (Prov 5:3; Song 4:11; 5:5, 13; Amos 9:13; Joel 3:18). So when Micah suggests that popular *preaching* is like being dripped on with wine and strong drink (2:11), the text is playing on the connection of the image of the "preacher" (*mattif*) and what it is that such preaching typically produces. It "oozes with sappy sweetness or with intoxicating and numbing alcohol." It is very likely, I think, that when Micah applies the verb *nataf*, "preach," to what it is he is doing, he is applying the technical term for "prophesying" to his own activity. He is not trying to distance himself from prophetic action. He is rather indicating his own participation in it. His preaching, however, refuses to "drip" the typical sort of sentimental drivel, the same old sticky-sweet clichés that that people are expecting to hear in such preaching. His preaching will refuse to back away from the hard realities of the judgment that awaits the people.

Style and Themes in Micah

Whether or not Micah was what we would call a preacher, he certainly was what we would call a poet, and his literary style is filled with the power of poetic language and image. Consider the dramatic alliteration that so fills 1:10-16 with power, as Micah surveys the towns of the Shephelah southwest of Jerusalem, in the neighborhood of his hometown of Moresheth:

"Tell it not in Gath, weep not at all" (*begat 'al-taggidu, bako 'al-tibku*)

"In Beth-leaphrah roll yourselves in the dust" (*bebet le'afrah 'afar hithpallashi*)

"The inhabitants of Zaanan do not come forth" (*yoshebet tse'anan lo yatse'ah*)

"Harness the steeds to the chariots, inhabitants of Lachish" (. . . *larekesh yoshebet lakish*)

"The houses of Achzib shall be a deceptive lie" (*botte 'akzib le'akzab*)

"I will again bring a conqueror upon you, O Mareshah" (*'od hayyoresh 'abi lak yoshebet mareshah*).

This is the skill of an orator whose words fall like a hammer rather than drip like honey or wine.

Micah explores the themes already introduced by Amos and Hosea, once again showing that one cannot separate concerns about worshiping the right God from concerns about worshiping God rightly. Like Hosea, he condemns the religious practices of idolatry, making the connection between religious apostasy and adultery (1:7). But Micah's biggest guns are, as in Amos and Isaiah, saved for the corrupt and unjust social practices of those wealthy patrons of power who "devise wickedness and evil deeds upon their beds," who confiscate private land and homes (2:1-2). It is especially these leaders who stand under judgment, those who are responsible for justice, but yet who cannibalize their own people, skinning them and cooking them up in a stew of injustice (3:1-3). These leaders "hate justice and pervert all fairness; they build Zion with blood and Jerusalem with injustice" (3:9-10). Micah condemns the corrupt business practices ("wicked scales and deceitful weights") and the social violence perpetrated by the rich (6:11-12).

In the midst of this severe social critique, Micah imagines a courtroom scene in which God is bringing his people to trial (6:3-4): "O my people, what have I done to you? In what have I wearied you (*umah hel'etika*)? Answer me! For I brought you up (*ki he'elitika*) from the land of Egypt." In this pointed play on words, God contrasts in the sharpest terms what the people are accusing God of and what it is that God really did. Then in 6:5 God turns to invite the people to remember their past—Balak, Balaam, Shittim, Gilgal— in order that they may know the *tsidqot YHWH*. These are names that rehearse certain events in Israel's life that point to Israel's many failures. Curiously, the phrase *tsidqot YHWH* here often is translated as "saving acts" of the Lord, as though what happened at these places was "good news," as though the reference to Shittim and Gilgal simply rehearsed the wonderful crossing of the Jordan River led by God's grace in triumphalistic fashion. But this is incorrect. The phrase needs to be translated not as "saving acts" but rather as "acts of *judgment*" of the Lord, because all of these places were locations where the people encountered their own brokenness and evil. The temptation to rush to salvation and the gospel and to the triumphalism of religious optimism, the desire to avoid the language of judgment and sin, may be characteristic of the way we prefer to read Scripture. But it undercuts the fact that we have, in Micah 6:1-5, a judgment oracle precisely in the form of a legal case, a "prophetic lawsuit" (Hebrew *rib*, vv. 1-2).

In responding to such judgment, we might think the situation hopeless and God's demands unreasonable or impossible (thousands of rams, myriads of rivers of oil, the sacrifice of a firstborn child!). The response to such judgment, however, is the simple reduction of human response to its fundamental level: "He has showed you, O mortal, what is good. And what does the Lord require of you but to do justice, and to love kindness, and to walk humbly with your God?" (6:8).

The Voice of Restoration

Though the historical Micah may have been a thoroughgoing prophet of judgment, in its final canonical shape the book nevertheless focuses on divine grace and restoration. The note of salvation is already sounded briefly in 2:12-13, but it is taken up more completely in chapters 4 and 5 and again in chapter 7. Though chapter 3 concludes with the reference to Jerusalem, the "mountain of the house," becoming "a heap of ruins and a wooded height," the image is immediately reversed in 4:1 as the promise is made that, in the latter days, "the mountain of the house of the Lord shall be established as the highest of the mountains," the goal of many nations who shall "flow" to it to hear the Torah and the word going forth from the city. Then follows a vision of universal peace, "swords to plowshares," of everyone sitting under vines and fig trees, of the lame and outcasts being gently gathered into Zion under God's rule, of the reversal of military power, so that even the powerful Assyrians will be defeated by the shepherds of Israel.

The book ends with a hymn of praise: "Who is a God like you, pardoning iniquity and passing over transgression?" (7:18). The phrase "Who is a God like you" (*mi-'el kamoka*) rehearses the name of this prophet: Micah, short for *mi-ke'el*, "Who is like God?" Micah of Moresheth stood opposed to the optimism of Isaiah. Living in the midst of a militarism that spread like a cancer from Jerusalem, Micah spoke in harsh terms of God's judgment on the excesses of wealth and military power. But even though we might wish that Micah's word would have ceased at 3:12 with the final word of judgment, the book goes on to speak also of divine reversal, including military reversal. The prophet's very name, Micah—"Who is like . . . ?"—echoes in the final oracle of the book. "Who is like God," who again will have compassion, who will tread iniquity underfoot, who will cast all sin into the depths of the sea, who will show faithfulness and steadfast love? Who, indeed, is like God?

CHAPTER 7

Prophets in the Interim

Historical Background
to Zephaniah, Nahum, and Habakkuk

Following the Assyrian siege of Jerusalem, which failed in 701 B.C.E., King Hezekiah continued to reign for another fourteen years over Judah. We can assume that Hezekiah continued to take advantage of Assyria's international military setbacks and internal domestic turmoil, as a part of which the Assyrian king, Sennacherib, was ultimately assassinated in the year 681. During the remainder of his reign, Hezekiah apparently continued to press forward on his nationalistic plan to resist Assyrian domination and to centralize tighter national control around the royal administration in Jerusalem. Hezekiah died in 687 B.C.E. and was succeeded by his son Manasseh.

The impression from reading the account of the Deuteronomistic Historian in 2 Kings 21:1-18 is that the difference between Hezekiah and his son was like night and day, black and white, good and evil. There is no hint in this account that Manasseh had any socially redeeming qualities at all. He immediately reversed his father's policies, subjected himself once again to the Assyrians, reinstituted every single cultic aberration that his father had cleaned out, and made the streets of Jerusalem run red with the blood of injustice. In fact, the

Deuteronomistic Historian blames Manasseh for single-handedly unleashing such a torrent of apostasy and evil upon Judah that its fate was sealed. Nothing in the world, not even the attempts at reform of the heroic King Josiah, would be able to turn the tide of destruction that was now fixed because of Manasseh (2 Kgs 23:26-27).

However, the matter appears to be not so simple. Manasseh came to the throne fully six years before Sennacherib was assassinated in an Assyrian palace coup. We can only assume that such chaos at the Assyrian capital indicated a continuing lack of control over the western nations and that, in fact, Manasseh's first years were characterized by continued attempts to assert Judah's independence in the face of this progressive disintegration of Assyrian internal affairs.

The account of Manasseh's reign in the Chronicler's History is very informative. According to 2 Chronicles 33:1-20, Manasseh's reign was marked by two different phases. The first phase (33:1-9) was a period of severe religious apostasy in which Manasseh utterly reversed his father's reform measures. Because of this apostasy, God punished Manasseh by sending an Assyrian invasion, as a result of which Manasseh himself was taken prisoner to appear before the Assyrian king. This jolt prompted Manasseh to repent, which in turn resulted in God restoring Manasseh to Jerusalem. Upon this restoration, Manasseh entered phase two and obeyed God by refortifying the city with walls and garrisoned troops and by conducting his own religious reform movement (33:10-17). The difficulty with this scenario is, however, that the Assyrians would certainly not have sent Manasseh back to Jerusalem only to have Manasseh rebuild its walls and fortifications and resupply its military defenses. It is precisely the report of these measures that would have prompted an Assyrian invasion and that would have been regarded as a rebellious nationalistic attempt to resist Assyrian dominance. The Chronicler's account is so tendentious that it could not possibly represent an accurate historical record.

Rather than assume that the first part of Manasseh's reign was characterized by overthrowing Hezekiah's anti-Assyrian policy, that Manasseh was then taken captive to Babylon, and that the second part of his reign was characterized by reinstating his father's policies, it is likely that we should reverse the scenario. It is only logical to assume that Manasseh *began* his reign by continuing his father's anti-Assyrian policies in the face of Assyria's continuing problems with its Babylonian provinces to the south and with its internal dissension leading to

Sennacherib's assassination. Once the new king, Esarhaddon, was on the throne and able to consolidate power, however, and once the "Babylonian problem" was under control, the Assyrians were once again able to reassert control over Judah, hauling Manasseh off and forcing him to submit. It was the second half of his reign, following his submission to the Assyrians under Esarhaddon, during which Manasseh would have been forced to give up his nationalistic measures of cultic reform and military expansion and submit to being a vassal of Assyria. In other words, it seems likely that Manasseh successfully pursued a reformist and nationalistic policy similar to his father for a number of years. When faced by a resurgent Assyria, however, he had no choice but to capitulate to the hard political realities of foreign domination and reinstitute the cultic and social policies incumbent on vassals of the great King Esarhaddon.

Within this context appear three prophetic figures who are among the briefer of the minor prophets: Zephaniah, Nahum, and Habakkuk. All three inhabit these interim years between Isaiah and Jeremiah, between the consolidation of Assyrian control over Judah during the reign of Manasseh and its final defeat at the hands of Babylon. As we will discuss in the next section, Assyria began to suffer fatal blows with the death of King Ashurbanipal in 627 B.C.E., and the capitals of Ashur and Nineveh finally fell to the Babylonians in 614 and 612 B.C.E., respectively. It is during these interim years, leading up to the final collapse of Assyria, that these three prophetic figures appear on history's stage. All three in their own way seek to understand these events within the context of God's plans for Judah.

Zephaniah and God's Universal Judgment

Though all three of these interim prophets appear on the scene shortly before Assyria's final demise, Zephaniah seems to be the earliest, as there is no specific indication that Assyria's cities were as yet under attack. Furthermore, Zephaniah's oracles against Judah suggest that religious apostasy was rampant and the temple administration itself was suspect, issues that would make sense given the fact that Manasseh spent the second part of his reign under tight Assyrian control, affecting even the practices of temple cult (Zeph 1:4-6). Assyrian pressure even had an effect on the way Judah's officials dressed as symbolic of their servitude to their suzerain (1:8). Under Assyrian domination, a sense of fatalism had apparently set in that regarded the power of Yahweh as no match for that of the Assyrian gods. Yahweh could do neither good nor ill and had, in their estimation, become irrelevant to unfolding historical events (1:12).

Zephaniah's judgment against Judah, however, was set within the context of universal judgment against all the nations of the earth. In a clever play on words, Zephaniah combined two different themes to depict this pending universal conflagration: that of the "flood" that wiped all life from the earth, and that of the celebration of the "Feast of Ingathering" (or the Feast of Booths), which may have been going on at the precise time that Zephaniah issued his oracles. In 1:2-3 these themes collide as the vocabulary of "gathering for removal" (*'asif*), a term used for Israel's major fall festival, is now employed to describe the effect of the universal flood:

> "I will utterly gather together for removal (*'asof 'asef*) everything from the face of the earth," says Yahweh. "I will gather for removal (*'asef*) humankind and beast . . . , birds of the air and the fish of the sea. . . . I will cut off humankind from the face of the earth," says Yahweh.

Within this vision of universal conflagration, Zephaniah moves through an array of nations who will experience God's judgment: not only Jerusalem but the Philistine cities of Gaza, Ashkelon, Ashdod, and the sea coast (2:1-7); Moab (2:8-11); Ethiopia (2:12); and finally, as of critical importance, Assyria and its imperial and exultant capital, Nineveh, which boasts: "I am and there is none else" (2:13-15). This universal judgment is restated in 3:8, as the gathered nations and kingdoms will suffer God's indignation and the heat of divine anger: "for in the fire of my jealous wrath all the earth shall be consumed." The movement of history during this period was so momentous that only the language of universal flood and conflagration could possibly capture the spirit of desperation that the prophet must have felt.

After the smoke from this universal conflagration clears, after the floodwaters that gathered together all life to destroy it from the face of the earth have abated, God will leave "a people humble and lowly, who shall seek refuge in the name of Yahweh" (Zeph 3:11-13). In a final restatement of the central theme, the language of destruction and divine removal is reversed as once again the language of the Feast of

Ingathering is invoked for Judah's salvation: God "will exult over you with loud singing. The grieving of the day of festival I have removed (*'asafti*) from you" (Zeph 3:17-18). The joy of the festive celebration would be restored to the Feast of Ingathering, and the Assyrians would take their deserved place in this coming universal judgment of the nations.

Nahum and the Drums of War

If Assyria's destruction was envisioned by Zephaniah as only one part, albeit an important one, of universal conflagration, Nahum focused exclusively on Assyria's pending destruction. This singular focus on Nineveh is clear from the very beginning: "An oracle concerning Nineveh" (Nah 1:1). We might think it chauvinistic and even unbiblical that a prophet should focus oracles against the enemies of state rather than against his own people. But recall that the origins of prophecy lay, at least to some extent, in the phenomenon of "war prophecy" discussed earlier. Such oracles had long been connected to the very social function of prophecy. And even prophets whom we might not associate with nationalistic chauvinism produced such oracles against the nations. We saw already that Amos had such oracles (Amos 1–2), even though they were part of a program leading up to the critical judgment against Israel itself. But other prophets also had collections of such oracles: Isaiah 13–24, Jeremiah 46–50, and Ezekiel 25–32 all have such collections. We should not assume, then, that Nahum was any more chauvinistic than any of the others. Such was a typical function and form of ancient Near Eastern prophecy.

What is so interesting about Nahum is not necessarily what he says as the manner in which he says it. For Nahum, the destruction of Nineveh is so near that he can feel it, taste it, and certainly *hear* it. The drums of war sound loudly in Nahum's prophecies concerning the imminent invasion of Nineveh and the destruction of its proud gates and walls. Hebrew poetry is most frequently expressed in a trimeter verse in which each line has three beats, there being generally two parallel lines to complete an idea. Normally, then, Hebrew poetry sounds more like a waltz in what musicians would call "six-eight" time (six beats to the measure, the eighth note receiving a beat). A lilting and soft style of expression, such poetry is common in Israel's poetic and prophetic literature. Sometimes a line of four beats can replace that of three beats, but it is relatively uncommon. What is unique about the book of Nahum is that the prophet employs a shocking meter that is two beats per line, over and over again, like a hammer pounding on an anvil. This poetic style, though more difficult to detect in translation, is nevertheless still apparent. Consider the poetic style of 2:1-9:

> Man the ramparts, watch the road;
> gird your loins; collect all your strength. . . .
> The chargers prance. . . .
> They gleam like torches, they dart like lightning.
> The officers are summoned, they stumble as they go,
> they hasten to the wall. The mantelet is set up . . . ,
> the palace trembles . . . its slave women led away,
> moaning like doves, beating their breasts.
> Nineveh is a pool, its waters depleted, away they run.
> "Stop! Stop!"—but none turn around.
> "Plunder the silver, plunder the gold!"

This is nothing like normal Hebrew poetry! When reading this poetry, one can smell the sweat of horses and feel the ground shaking from the passing of the marching troops as the war drums pound out the march cadence. A similar startling cadence is used in 3:2-3:

> The crack of whip and rumble of wheel,
> galloping horse and bounding chariot!
> Horsemen charging
> flashing sword, glittering spear
> hosts of slain
> heaps of corpses, dead bodies no end.

Nahum's oracle against the pending military onslaught of Nineveh is not simply a theoretical vision. It is an existential reality, sucking the audience into its sights, smells, and sounds. Similar poetic power is seen in such outbursts as that of 2:10, where the prophet foresees the destruction of the city: "Desolate! Desolation and ruin!" (*buqah umebuqah umebullaqah*). The words of the Assyrians, laying siege to Jerusalem in the previous century, may still have hung in the air like acrid smoke. The Assyrian official, the Rabshakeh, asked the Jerusalem officials, "Where were the gods of Hamath and Arpad?

Where were the gods of Sepharvaim, Hena, and Ivvah? Have they delivered Samaria out of my hand? Who among all the gods of the countries have delivered their countries out of my hand, that the Lord should deliver Jerusalem out of my hand?" (2 Kgs 18:33-35). "Behold, you have heard what the kings of Assyria have done to all lands, destroying them utterly. And shall you be delivered?" (2 Kgs 19:11). Now God has a question for Assyria: "Are you better than Thebes that sat by the Nile, with water around her, her rampart a sea and water her wall?" (Nah 3:8). The Assyrians themselves had captured Thebes, the southern capital of Egypt, earlier in the century. Could they not even learn a lesson from their own history? Water does not make good walls! So Nineveh, itself surrounded by the waters of the Tigris River on the west and a series of moats on the east, would have to learn the hard way. It would fare no better than did Thebes.

Some seventy or eighty years earlier, Isaiah had sensed that Assyria, the "rod of Yahweh's anger," would itself become the object of Yahweh's wrath. But the image was very blurry. Now, some generations later, the picture was coming into increasingly sharper focus, and Nineveh's days were numbered. If one listened carefully, one could already hear the thudding of drumbeats off in the distance.

Habakkuk and "Keeping the Faith"

The book of Habakkuk likely also has its setting during this same interim period when the fortunes of empires were set to change. Though not as clearly stated, Habakkuk 1:5-6 suggests that the Babylonians are being roused for their march across the earth. It was the Babylonians who defeated Assyria by destroying its capitals at Ashur and Nineveh in 614 and 612 b.c.e., respectively. Most, therefore, assume that the pending destruction of Assyria is also the historical backdrop for the prophecy of Habakkuk.

What is peculiar about the book of Habakkuk, however, is the form the book takes: a series of two oracles that seek to address the prophet's haunting question: Why do the righteous seem to suffer while the wicked prosper? (see 1:2-4, 13). The prophet addresses this challenge to God, then "takes his stand on the tower to watch" for God's answer (2:1). The answers that come are themselves unsettling, or at least ought to be. The first response is that God is not inattentive to human cries of need or to failures of justice. Watch the international news, for God is at work in strange ways. The Babylonians are the answer! (1:5-6). Of course, if the answer is Babylon, then we perhaps need to reconsider the question, or at least our assumptions about the question. Similarly, the second response is to wait and, in the meantime, live lives of trust (2:2-4). The rest of the oracle is comprised of a series of woe oracles, which in the context can be understood to relate to Assyria, who "plundered many nations" (2:8), "cutting off many peoples" (2:10), was the city "built with bloodshed" (2:12), which made its neighbors "drink the cup of his wrath" (2:15). But there is not a lot of specificity to this language, allowing it to have broader ranges of meanings than simply those relating to Assyrian politics.

The last chapter of Habakkuk is a separate rhetorical unit, a "prayer" (*tefillah*, i.e., complaint or lament) of Habakkuk, an appeal for God to "remember mercy" (3:2). It uses mythological language of God the divine warrior, accompanied by his weapons "pestilence" and "plague," who has come to defeat once again the chaos symbolized by "sea" and "rivers." As in the divine summons to "wait" (*hakah*) for divine relief amid a life of trust (2:3), the book concludes with the confident prayer that the prophetic speaker will "lie down and rest" (*nuah*) in God's action of deliverance (3:16). Even though there is no evidence to bolster hope, even though there is no logical argument to convince anyone, even though all the evidence seems to point in the opposite direction, the prophet/petitioner will nevertheless rejoice in the saving power of God (3:17-19).

Habakkuk's vision of the righteous life lived in such trust is, of course, at the root of Christian hope that "the righteous shall live through faith." It is an unfortunate misunderstanding of the text, which under the influence of Protestant fervor, takes this phrase to mean that eternal life comes to the one who is made righteous by faith. The translation of the RSV was not helpful at this point: "He who through faith is righteous shall live" (Rom 1:17; Gal 3:11). To understand the text as a recipe for how to secure eternal life stands the word of Habakkuk on its head. Rather, the righteous person is called to live a life of trust (*'emunah*). They must be able to say "Amen!" to divine realities that are as strange as accepting the fact that Babylon is the answer to our prayers. If one is living during a time when the fortunes of empires are set to change, in an interim period when everything seems uncertain, this is not a bad message.

CHAPTER 8

Jeremiah
and the Reforms of Josiah

◆

Jeremiah in Broad Historical Perspective

Prophecy in preexilic Israel reached its culmination in the prophetic ministry of Jeremiah. Though not all of the material in the book can with certainty be ascribed to the prophet Jeremiah, scholars generally recognize that much of it can, especially the oracles contained in chapters 1–25. Furthermore, the narratives about Jeremiah—whether ascribed to his secretary Baruch or to a later editor—bear a close relationship to the life of this prophet from the village of Anathoth. The collection of oracles against the nations, gathered together in chapters 46–51, also are closely connected to the Jeremiah tradition, and the core of this material most assuredly comes from the prophet himself or his close circle. The book of Jeremiah is by far the most extensive collection of preexilic oracles available, and the biographical sketches provided are unparalleled in any other source. We will discuss later the issues of how the book is structured and what it means to have such a portrait of the prophet as provided by the book. The critical issue to begin our conversation is the historical context of Jeremiah's prophetic ministry.

We saw earlier that the ministries of Zephaniah, Nahum, and Habakkuk took place in the interim between the renewal of Assyrian domination over Judah during the reign of King Manasseh and the final failure of Assyrian statehood with the Babylonian assault on its capital cities, Ashur and Nineveh, in 614–612 B.C.E. When precisely during this period these three prophets appeared is unclear, though internal evidence would suggest closer to 614 B.C.E. If so, Jeremiah's ministry may have begun earlier than theirs, and he may therefore have been an earlier contemporary who bracketed their ministries with his own long prophetic career. But whereas their ministries were mostly aimed against the Assyrian threat and its final downfall, Jeremiah's was directed more toward the internal political and social realities racking Judah and Jerusalem.

The Rise of King Josiah

Manasseh most likely began his reign with every intention of pursuing his father's (Hezekiah) anti-Assyrian revolt, including its accompanying nationalistic cultic reform movement. But when the Assyrians overcame their internal chaos and managed to put down the "Babylonian problem," they once again moved back into the Levant, took Manasseh captive, and forced him to submit to their Assyrian oversight and control, bringing with it a reversion to the cultic aberrations so detested by the Deuteronomistic program. Manasseh was succeeded by his son, Amon. Amon continued his father's policies of subservience to the Assyrians (2 Kgs 21:19-22), but he reigned only two years before his own royal servants assassinated him. One can only suspect that these servants represented a movement in the palace to switch foreign policies and revolt against the Assyrians. The Deuteronomistic Historian indicates, however, that the coup failed. The "people of the land" killed the conspirators and placed Amon's young son, Josiah, on the throne.

Who were these "people of the land" and what was their stake in the matter? Many scholars see in the action of these "people of the land" a reform-minded nationalistic attempt to change the existing political policies. I believe, however, that the opposite is the case. The "people of the land," particularly if they were non-Jerusalemite residents of Judah, leading elders representing the outlying rural areas, knew that whenever foreign forces invaded it was rural Judah that suffered the brunt of the attack. As such, they were not interested in a nationalistic uprising against Assyria that could bring Assyrian troops once again to lay siege against their less well fortified towns and villages. The "people of the land" wanted to maintain the existing foreign policy of submission to Assyria in order to keep the Assyrian armies at bay. It was for this reason that they put down the coup attempt against Amon, killed the conspirators who wanted to change political direction, and placed the young Josiah on his father's throne, assuming that they would control him during his minority years.

In these dangerous circumstances, Josiah came to the throne in 640 B.C.E. when he was only eight years old. As was typically the case, Josiah would have been under the supervision of a political mentor during these years, and this mentor—representing the interests of the "people of the land"—undoubtedly kept Josiah under control and maintained the pro-Assyrian foreign policy reinstituted by Manasseh and maintained by Amon.

The Reform Movement of King Josiah

According to the account of Josiah's reign given in the Deuteronomistic History, nothing significant happened until the eighteenth year of his reign (622/621 B.C.E.), when Josiah decided to remodel the Jerusalem temple. During this remodeling, a document was found, referred to as "the book of the law" (*sefer hattorah,* 2 Kgs 22:8). The finding of this document prompted the beginning of a reform movement, including a reform of the temple cult, outlying worship sites, and the institution of the Passover Festival (23:1-25).

If one compares this account with that of the Chronicler, however, it appears that the beginning of the reform movement was much more complicated. In 2 Chronicles 34:3 we learn that a major shift was already in the plans in Josiah's eighth regnal year, fully ten years prior to anything reported in the Deuteronomistic History. It was in this year, 632/631 B.C.E., that Josiah reached his "majority" (he turned sixteen) and "began to seek the God of David his father." This is a clear indication that as soon as Josiah was old enough to exert his independence from his mentors, he began to fashion a counterstrategy for foreign policy. Furthermore, we learn that the reform movement began already in his twelfth regnal year (2 Chr 34:3-7), that is, in 628/627 B.C.E., six years before that reported in the Deuteronomistic History. Although the Chronicler's History was written considerably later than the Deuteronomistic History and often pursues its own interests, most scholars believe that at this point the Chronicler's History is correct and ought to be followed.

The Role of the "Deuteronomic Code" in the Reform Movement

Assuming that the Chronicler was correct, what do we learn about the nature of this Josianic reform? Two points are important. The first has to do with the reasons for the temple remodeling, and the second has to do with the function of the book of the law in the unfolding reform.

The Deuteronomistic History would lead us to believe that Josiah decided to remodel the temple for no apparent reason, and that it was only as a result of the finding of the book of the law that the reform movement thereafter began. But if the reform movement began already in 628 B.C.E., it had been going on in full force for six years by the time the temple was remodeled. In this case it is clear that the remodeling of the temple was not simply an attempt to reinforce its sagging walls or restructure its design. Rather, it was itself part of the reform movement. The temple in Jerusalem was a part of the royal complex, the country's central national shrine, embodying its theopolitical identity. As such, it was the chief cultic symbol of Israel's foreign policy. As a part of the ongoing reform movement, Josiah commissioned it to be overhauled as representative of his shift in political alliances. His reform movement was an integral part of his newfound anti-Assyrian policy and his decision to revolt against Assyrian domination.

If we assume that the reform movement was in full force already in 628 B.C.E., then the finding of the book of the law in 622—six years later—could clearly not have been the driving force for the reform. Indeed, if the Chronicler's History is correct, the reform was completely over by the time the law book was found. Jerusalem and Judah had already been "purged" (2 Chr 34:3-5) and the reforms had been carried to the north, where attempts were made apparently to consolidate Judean control over the former tribal areas of Israel, currently Assyrian provinces (34:6-7). After the book of the law was found (34:8-28), the only thing that remained was the reestablishment of the covenant itself, under the influence of the newly discovered book, and the celebration of the Passover (34:29—35:19). In other words, the only effect that the discovery of the book of the law had on the reform movement was to give what was essentially a political anti-Assyrian revolt a more specifically theological rationale and concluding ritual action.

Reading the account of the Deuteronomistic History, one would think that the entire reform movement was based on and sustained by the finding of the book of the law. Why was the book promoted to being of such fundamental importance by the Deuteronomistic Historian? Consider the very name given to this historical work: the *Deuteronomistic* History. It is given this name because its writing is based on the principles established in the book of Deuteronomy and the major theological commitments expressed therein. The Deuteronomistic History is the child of the Deuteronomic program and is its clearest literary expression. The book of the law found by Josiah is generally thought by scholars to be the book of Deuteronomy or part of it, perhaps chapters 12–26 or 12–28. If so, one can see why the Deuteronomistic Historian would have promoted the discovery of this book to the central position. It was, according to the Deuteronomistic Historian, not simply an afterthought. It had to have been, according to the Deuteronomistic Historian, the primary cause that forced Josiah to redirect his entire program and institute the reform movement from the very beginning. If, for the Chronicler, the book was found only after the end of the reform, it then gave the reform a concluding theological or ritual completion (covenant renewal and institution of the Passover). In the Deuteronomistic Historian's view, however, the book (Deuteronomy) *had* to have had a central function: it was, in the Deuteronomistic Historian's view, the very reason for the reform's initiation and continued existence.

The Question of a "Josianic" Ministry of Jeremiah

A critical question in Jeremiah studies is when Jeremiah's ministry began. The superscription of the book indicates that his prophetic career began during the days of Josiah, specifically in the thirteenth year of his reign (ca. 627 B.C.E., Jer 1:1-2). In current scholarship, however, a major scholarly position has developed that the year 627 B.C.E.

did not mark the date of the onset of his career but rather the date of his birth. Linking the reference to Josiah's thirteenth regnal year (1:2) to the language regarding Jeremiah's birth (1:4-5), these scholars suggest that Jeremiah was only *born* in 627 b.c.e., that he was too young to have exercised any ministry under Josiah, and it was only upon Josiah's death in 609 b.c.e.—Jeremiah now being eighteen years of age—that he began his career under Josiah's successor, King Jehoiakim.

The argument for this late date for Jeremiah's career is usually based on a number of observations. First, these scholars argue that no oracles seem to be dated to the period of Josiah. Second, they contend that Jeremiah is silent on the Josianic reform movement and only reacts to it after the fact. Third, they assume that Jeremiah's reference to a "foe from the north" would be meaningless prior to 605 b.c.e. when the Babylonians descended on the Philistine plain, as there would be no good candidate for such a foe prior to that. Finally, they insist that Jeremiah's call to celibacy (16:1-4) must be dated to 601 b.c.e. or later, and would therefore only make sense if Jeremiah were in the prime of life (born in 627) rather than an older man (having begun his ministry in 627).

All of these assumptions, however, are problematic. As for the assumption that no oracles seem to be dated to the period of Josiah, the reference given in 3:6 explicitly dates this oracle to "the days of King Josiah," as does the clear reference in 36:2. Other oracles presuppose that Assyria is still in existence (2:18), and many oracles in the "Book of Consolation" (chaps. 30–33) appear to address the northern tribes of Israel. This appeal to Israel is likely evidence of the sort of Josianic hope for control of the northern territories of Israel that we discussed above. Other texts, such as 25:3, certainly assume that Jeremiah's ministry began in 627 b.c.e.

The argument that Jeremiah is silent on the Josianic reform movement is impossible to defend. Jeremiah thought very highly of Josiah, who was the model of the just king (22:15-16). Indeed, Jeremiah is so deeply steeped in the Deuteronomic traditions that shaped the book of the law that scholars have a difficult time determining where Jeremiah's writing leaves off and the writing of the Deuteronomistic editors who shaped the book begins. The clearest indication of a deep and abiding connection between Jeremiah and the Josianic reform movement is the relationship that Jeremiah sustained with the family of Shaphan, as will be seen below.

The question of what nation could be considered the "foe from the north" (e.g., 4:5-8; 6:1, 22; 10:22; 25:9) in an early dating, prior to the Babylonian incursion into the Levant in 605 B.C.E., is more complicated. The Assyrians had begun a final plunge into disaster following the death of King Ashurbanipal in 627 B.C.E. A period of increasing weakness led eventually to the defeat of its capitals, Ashur and Nineveh, in the years 614 and 612 B.C.E., respectively. For their part, the Babylonians were not able to qualify for such an honorable title for several more years. So who could this "foe" be? The desire to find a specific nation (the Scythians are often proposed) overlooks the extent to which this language of "the foe from the north" is a mythological symbol that does not depend on specific events of history. Babylon was only *one* of the nations from the north (25:26, where Babylon = Sheshach), and certainly the reputation of the Assyrians lived on in Judean memories. Ashurbanipal, the last of the powerful kings of Assyria, had died only in 627 B.C.E., and certainly no one had written the Assyrians off yet. In the end, the concept of "the north" was itself so personified in Israelite mythology that it took on a personality of its own (e.g., Isa 14:31; 41:25; Zeph 2:13; Ezek 1:4; 23:24). The personification of "the north" as an ominous direction from which trouble comes was part of the consciousness of Israelite thought and did not require a specific nation to give it a concrete expression.

Jeremiah's call to celibacy is only a problem if one insists that Jeremiah 16:1-4 must be taken literally and must be dated to a period by which Jeremiah would be an older man. But there is no indication whatsoever that the text must be dated to any specific time. The context within which the oracle is placed presumes a dating generally during the reign of King Jehoiakim (609–597 B.C.E.), but the placement of this oracle here has more to do with its literary theme relating to a drought and, more specifically, to "bridegroom and bride" (16:9) than to any imagined literal meaning or chronological order, as we will see in the next discussion.

None of the arguments that seek to support a late date for the beginning of Jeremiah's ministry is convincing. It is best, in my opinion, to adopt the traditional view that takes the note in the superscription literally. Jeremiah's prophetic ministry began in the year 627 B.C.E., King Josiah's thirteenth regnal year. This was an auspicious moment in history for several reasons. As mentioned earlier, Ashurbanipal died in that year, and it must have been clear that momentous changes were about to overtake world politics. Josiah had just begun his cultic purge of Judah and Jerusalem in the previous year. If we estimate that Jeremiah was eighteen years of age when beginning his career, that would place his birth in about 645 B.C.E. Jeremiah was a young boy during the final years of the reign of Manasseh, became a teenager during Josiah's minority years, and watched as an adolescent as Josiah's policies began to shift in a nationalistic and reformist direction. Jeremiah's ministry, beginning in 627, can be seen as part of the same spirit that motivated Josiah's Deuteronomic reform the previous year. Indeed, Jeremiah may well have been one of the leading proponents of the reform, giving early support to Josiah's efforts in his bold preaching against precisely the sort of cultic corruption that Josiah sought to root out.

Jeremiah and the Family of Shaphan

The argument that Jeremiah had no relationship to Josiah's reform movement is betrayed by the fact that one of Jeremiah's clearest political alliances was with the reform-minded family of Shaphan. Shaphan himself had been instrumental in the reform's progress, and was certainly one of the royal officials most encouraging Josiah to pursue the nationalistic policy. It was Shaphan, Josiah's royal secretary, who was entrusted with the temple reform (2 Kgs 22:3-7), and it was Shaphan who presented to Josiah the book of the law upon its discovery (22:8-10).

Members of this reformist family keep appearing in the book of Jeremiah as his closest political allies and colleagues. It is Ahikam, the son of Shaphan, who intervenes to save Jeremiah's life when he is on public trial for treason (Jer 26:24). It is Gemariah, another son of Shaphan, together with Micaiah, a grandson, who appeal to Jeremiah and Baruch to hide after the public reading of his first written scroll of oracles (36:19). It is Elasah, another son of Shaphan, who delivers Jeremiah's letter to Babylon (29:3). Finally, it is Gedaliah, a grandson of Shaphan and the son of Ahikam, who becomes Jeremiah's protector following the final collapse of Judah and Jerusalem (39:14; 40:6).

The family of Shaphan was one of the most thoroughly reform-minded families among the Jerusalem officials. It is this fact that accounts for the appointment of Gedaliah as governor over Judah by the Babylonians when they finally took Jerusalem and pacified the countryside. This is one family who all along had appealed to the king to capitulate to the Babylonian forces. Such a policy might seem counter to the nationalistic reform of Josiah. Recall, however, that that reform movement was born as an anti-Assyrian political expression. Interestingly, Josiah himself was faced with a critical decision whether to support the Assyrians or the Babylonians once the Babylonians had destroyed the Assyrian capitals of Ashur and Nineveh. Josiah chose to support the Babylonians. He showed his alliance with the Babylonians by trying to stop an Egyptian army that was heading northward through Israel on its way to assist the Assyrian army in its final stand against the Babylonian army. Josiah did not want this assistance to succeed, so he attacked the Egyptian army at the city of Megiddo in northern Israel. In this battle Josiah was killed. But Josiah had made clear that he preferred a Babylonian power to that of Assyria. It is not that Josiah was pro-Babylonian, nor was the reformist family of Shaphan pro-Babylonian. But the issues were complicated in those days, and the relatively positive sentiments shown by Josiah toward the Babylonians carried through into the policies of his secretary, Shaphan, into Shaphan's family, and, through them, into the message of the greatest prophet in preexilic Israel, Jeremiah, the prophet from Anathoth.

CHAPTER 9

The Structure of the Book of Jeremiah

Jeremiah and the Fall of Judah

Although Josiah's reign was long and prosperous, he was killed in 609 B.C.E. as a result of attempting to keep the Egyptian army from going to the defense of the Assyrian army, which was staging its final stand against the Babylonians. After Josiah's death, Judah's remaining years were a whirlwind of political intrigue and disasters and a succession of kings who could not decide what sort of foreign policy to pursue. The "people of the land"—again apparently attempting to insert themselves into Judean politics—placed a younger son of Josiah on the throne by the name of Jehoahaz (= Shallum). But Shallum was quickly removed from power by the Egyptians, who in the wake of their victory over Josiah had consolidated their control over Judah and Palestine. The Egyptians replaced Shallum with his older brother, Eliakim (= Jehoiakim). Within a few years, however, the Babylonians defeated the remnant of the Assyrian army at the city of Haran, then turned on the Egyptian relief effort, defeating them at Carchemish and again at Hamath. By 604 the Babylonians were in full control of the Levant, and King Jehoiakim had to realign his political alliances accordingly.

Jehoiakim harbored hopes for political independence, however, and attempted a revolt in a moment of what appeared to be Babylonian weakness. He badly miscalculated, however, and the Babylonian army laid siege to the cities of Judah. Jehoiakim, who had ruled since 609 B.C.E., died in 598 B.C.E., during the height of this siege, and left a bitter inheritance for his son, Jehoiachin. The first official business Jehoiachin had to administer was his surrender to the Babylonian army. Jehoiachin himself, along with a large number of the Judean leadership, intellectuals, and skilled artisans, was taken prisoner to various sites in Mesopotamia, marking what is referred to as the "first deportation" (597 B.C.E.). After taking Jehoiachin into exile, the Babylonians placed his uncle Zedekiah, a third son of King Josiah, on the throne. But Zedekiah too was badly advised by princes who dreamed of revolt. He wisely avoided participating in an attempted revolt by neighboring states in 594 B.C.E., but could not resist another attempt a few years later. In 589 B.C.E. he joined a larger conspiracy of nations to revolt against his Babylonian overlords. For the second time the Babylonians laid siege to the cities of Judah and finally to Jerusalem itself, and the city finally fell in 587 B.C.E. after a prolonged and desperate siege.

The book of Jeremiah thus is set against the tumultuous final years of Judean statehood under these kings: Shallum (Jehoahaz), Jehoiakim, Jehoiachin, and Zedekiah. After its final collapse and defeat at the hand of the Babylonians, Nebuchadnezzar, the king of Babylon, alternatingly referred to in the book of Jeremiah as Nebuchadrezzar (from the Babylonian *Nabu-kudurri-usur*), appointed Gedaliah as the Judean governor of Jehud, which was now a Babylonian province. Gedaliah was himself assassinated by a member of the Judean royal family in an apparent attempt once again to revolt and restart the monarchy under a Davidic king. But the Babylonians had too firm a control, and the only result of this attempted nationalistic uprising was to cause further turmoil in the land. It is in the midst of this turmoil that some of the residents remaining in Judah decided to flee for safety to Egypt, and they took Jeremiah with them as a virtual hostage. This is the last glimpse we have of Jeremiah, as he is being swept along to Egypt in these desperate times.

Basic Issues Concerning the Book

The book of Jeremiah is often regarded as an editorial disaster, containing little or no organization, a scattered collection of oracles that boggles attempts to discern any logical structure. Anyone who has read through the book in one sitting knows how daunting the task can be. Its oracles and stories move back and forth between the reigns of various kings so rapidly that one feels caught in a storm of time warps. References to the final kings of Judah are dizzying: Josiah (3:6), Zedekiah (21:1), Jehoiakim (25:1), Zedekiah (27:1), Jehoiakim (35:1), Zedekiah (37:1), Jehoiakim (45:1), and then all the way once again back to the Egyptian Pharaoh Neco, who was the general who defeated Josiah at Megiddo (46:2).

In addition to this dizzying chronological puzzle, a number of editorial notes seem to make no sense given their context and betray a heavy-handed editing of earlier material. For example, 25:13 refers in the third person to "this book, which Jeremiah prophesied." Such a note is utterly discordant with the context, in which Jeremiah himself speaks these words (cf. 25:3). Or consider 31:26, which suggests that this note concludes a sequence of dream visions that Jeremiah is reporting ("Thereupon I awoke and looked, and my sleep was pleasant to me"). Yet there is no logical opening to such a dream sequence, no satisfactory rhetorical clue as to where Jeremiah would have fallen asleep to have these dreams. These are but two examples of the rhetorical difficulties that confront one in attempting to understand the editorial history and logical structure of the book.

Another major problem that confronts scholars is the comparison of the Hebrew text of Jeremiah to the Greek translation, the Septuagint. No book presents such wide variances between these two editions as does the book of Jeremiah. Not only is the Hebrew text of Jeremiah considerably longer than the Greek text, it is ordered significantly differently. The most notable difference is that, whereas the existing Hebrew text (and our modern translations) locates the collected oracles against the nations at the end of the book in chapters 46–51, the Septuagint locates them following chapter 25 and rearranges the individual oracles. But there are also a myriad of less obvious differences that nonetheless reflect dramatically different editorial principles. The antiquity of the Hebrew text underlying the Septuagint is attested already in several Qumran manuscripts, demonstrating that both versions—in Hebrew—were in circulation by the end of the second century B.C.E. Scholars furiously debate which text is the original edition, and the book of Jeremiah presents the single case in which many scholars actually prefer the Septuagint over the Hebrew text as corresponding more closely to the earliest form of the book. Some scholars have gone so far as to argue that the Septuagint presents us with a more authentic picture of Jeremiah, whose stature as a prophet was considerably enhanced and exaggerated by the later edition represented by the existing Hebrew text. The idea that the Septuagint gives us a better view of the original Hebrew text of Jeremiah than does the present Hebrew text is probably overstated, but this issue remains a major difficulty in Jeremiah studies.

Jeremiah, Baruch, and the Deuteronomistic Editors

One of the most interesting features of the book of Jeremiah is that it gives us a glimpse of its own editorial history. Just as no other prophetic book gives us such a personal picture of the prophet himself, so no other prophetic book gives us such a wonderful depiction of the prophet's actual editorial work. Chapter 36 presents us with an astounding narrative concerning how it is that a "first edition" of the scroll of Jeremiah was produced, and hints about how a "second edition" replaced it. According to this tradition, Jeremiah commissioned his secretary, Baruch ben Neriah, to compile a collection of Jeremiah's prophetic oracles in the fourth year of the reign of King Jehoiakim (605 B.C.E.). This manuscript created such a stir among the leaders of Judah when it was read the following year that Jeremiah and Baruch were urged to go into protective hiding. Upon reading the scroll, Jehoiakim cut it into pieces, column by column, and burned it in his fireplace. After this first scroll had been destroyed, Jeremiah was commissioned to have Baruch create an expanded edition of the scroll containing what was in the first scroll along with "many similar words."

Many scholars suggest that the contents of this second edition formed the base of Jeremianic oracles now spread throughout chapters 1–25. The reference in 25:3 to this same duration of ministry (twenty-three years, i.e., 627–604 B.C.E.) and in 25:13 to "this book, which Jeremiah prophesied against all the nations," points to the same second scroll and to the oracles of chapters 1–25 as having developed around the core of these oracles copied by Baruch at the dictation of Jeremiah. Other scholars, however, suggest that the problem is not so easily resolved. After all, the reference in 25:13 to the oracles being directed "against all the nations" is in conflict with the fact that chapters 1–25 are oracles against Judah, even though these oracles are placed within a more universal context in 1:10. The comment regarding "all the nations" may suggest that the reference is not to the material in chapters 1–25 but rather to the oracles against the nations, which, if the Septuagint is correct, were originally located immediately following this remark. Furthermore, most scholars have long struggled with the difficult issue of how trustworthy the narrative biographical material in the book of Jeremiah is. Though more conservative scholars tend to ascribe this material to Baruch himself and trust it in large measure, most critical scholars have suggested that it is the work, rather, of later Deuteronomistic editors who had vested ideological and theological grounds for reshaping the material in order to create a certain "persona of the prophet" and his biographical data. If so, Jeremiah 36 itself might be suspect as being part of the persona created by the Deuteronomistic editors.

These problems are so complicated as to resist any simple or secure solution. Even those who see considerable Deuteronomistic editing at work in the Jeremiah material, however, suggest that Jeremiah's earliest oracles are certainly to be found within the material of chapters 1–25. Another problem, however, is that many scholars also assume that some of the oracles in chapters 30–31, sometimes referred to as the "Book of Consolation," also contain early Josianic oracles of Jeremiah addressed to Israel (i.e., the former northern kingdom) under the influence of Josiah's efforts at reunifying the northern and southern territories. For general purposes it is best to be aware of the possibility that chapter 36 provides a good indication of the sort of editorial activity by means of which the final book emerged, but also to be aware that the issue is almost certainly more complicated than that chapter might suggest. Where the work of Jeremiah, Baruch, and the later Deuteronomistic editors each begins and leaves off is a debated issue as perplexing as it is crucial.

Evidence of "Collections" of Material

Regardless of whether Baruch compiled a second scroll of Jeremianic oracles, or whether Deuteronomistic editors more gradually collected and assembled collections or oracles, there are indeed clues to suggest that the book consists of such smaller collections. For example, 14:1 opens a section "concerning the drought" (*'al-dibre habbatstsarot*). Though the theme is stated most literally in 14:1-6, it is pursued further with mention of "rain" and "showers" in 14:22 and with a restatement of the word "famine" again in 15:2. What Jeremiah finds to eat during this famine is "the words of God" (15:16), but God has become to Jeremiah like a "dried up wadi" (15:18). The word "famine" is recalled in 16:4, where the issue is now food for the animals as well as lack of food and drink during mourning and feasting rituals (16:7-8). The theme of "drought" is the backdrop for the imagery of 17:5-6 (shrubs in the desert, parched places of the wilderness, uninhabited salt land), the opposite of the water and fertility hinted at in verse 8. The term "drought" is used again in 17:8, and 17:13 identifies the "fountain of living water."

Similar collections of material focused on certain themes or catchwords can be seen in oracles relating to the royal house ("O King of Judah") in 22:1—23:8; a collection of oracles "concerning the prophets" (*lannebi'im*) is contained in 23:9-40; a collection of material concerned with correspondence sent to and received from the exiles is introduced in 29:1; 30:2 introduces a collection of oracles referred to as the "Book of Consolation" (see above); 25:13 suggests, as we have seen, that there was an early collection of oracles, perhaps those against the nations. The present book of Jeremiah is, in a sense, an anthology of collections of oracles that developed over time in the "Jeremiah tradition." The question, of course, is whether the final Deuteronomistic editor simply juxtaposed such collections with a minimum of his own work, expanding more fully the collection already gathered by Baruch, or whether it was the work of the final Deuteronomistic editor himself that created the various collections from smaller scattered traditions, whether written or oral. In other words, did this Deuteronomist function more like a publisher, an editor, or an author?

The Role of Rhetoric

The question of how much of the material in Jeremiah is to be attributed to Jeremiah, how much to Baruch, and how much to a later Deuteronomistic editor or school, or how the book came to its present shape, is worthy of considerable discussion. In the end, however, the more significant question is this: How did the final editor—whether Baruch or a much later Deuteronomistic editor—intend for the reader to read the material? Is it as chaotic and haphazard as most have suggested?

If one assumes that the editor had a scheme in mind for how the book was to be read, the scheme is to be seen in the basic rhetoric used to introduce major sections and subsections of the book. This rhetoric is not very exciting or spectacular, but the rhetoric of narrative often is not. Some sections in the book of Jeremiah are introduced with major introductory formulae that speak of the prophet in the third person and that use perfect verbs without a grammatical form known in Hebrew as a "*waw*-consecutive" (that is, a special form of the conjunction "and" that marks a continuing sequence of action). Such formulae can be seen, with slight variances, in phrases such as "The word that came to Jeremiah" (e.g., 1:2; 7:1; 11:1; 18:1; 25:1). Subsections of the book are introduced with other formulae, most of which refer to the prophet in the first person and which do depend on constructions using the common "*waw*-consecutive."

When taken together with the rhetoric of catchphrases, catchwords, and thematic units, the use and analysis of such introductory formulae can assist us in gaining an understanding of how the editorial process presented the book of Jeremiah for reading.

The Importance of the "Scroll of 605" in the Structure of the Book

At several key points in the book of Jeremiah, reference is made to what we discussed above as the "scroll of 605 B.C.E." What is of fundamental importance is that such a reference to this scroll appears in the book of Jeremiah at every point where there is a major shift in the chronological flow of the material, and nowhere else.

The first reference in the book of Jeremiah to a specific date is in 3:6, which dates the oracle to the reign of King Josiah. This reference indicates that the oracles in chapters 1–6 are intended by the editor to be read as Josianic oracles uttered by the prophet during the earliest part of his career. A major introductory formula is found at 7:1, "The word that came to Jeremiah" (*haddabar 'asher hayah 'el-yirmeyahu*), indicating the opening of a new section. There is no indication of chronological location given here, but most scholars assume that 7:1ff. is related to the identical event depicted in chapter 26. Since 26:1 is specifically dated to the "beginning of the reign of King Jehoiakim" (609 B.C.E.), it is generally assumed that 7:1 also marks a transition to the new king. Similarly, 21:1 uses a major introductory formula to introduce a series of oracles dated to the reign of King Zedekiah, as a part of which there is an review of royal history moving from Shallum (22:11-12) to Jehoiakim (22:13-23), Jehoiachin ("Coniah"; 22:24-30), and finally to Zedekiah (cf. 23:6, in which the name "Yahweh is our righteousness" [*YHWH tsidqenu*] is a play on the name Zedekiah [Hebrew *tsidqiyahu*, "Yahweh is my righteousness"]). In chapters 1–25 we thus have a movement in chronological order from Josiah to Shallum to Jehoiakim to Jehoiachin to Zedekiah. The first major chronological diversion occurs in 26:1, where suddenly we find ourselves back to the beginning of the reign of Jehoiakim. Note, however, that chapter 25 refers specifically to the "book of Jeremiah" that was written in 605/604 B.C.E., containing everything that Jeremiah had said from the beginning of his ministry in 627 down to the present moment. Reference to the scroll of 605 is critical to bringing this section to a conclusion before the chronology starts over again in 26:1.

Similarly, chapters 26–35 move chronologically from the reign of Jehoiakim (chap. 26) to Zedekiah (chaps. 27–34). Chapters 32–34 are located at the very end of the Babylonian siege while Jeremiah is confined by the royal officials in the "court of the guard." This material is dated very close to the final fall of Jerusalem in 587 B.C.E. Yet chapter 37 again forces a leap backward in history to a period at the beginning of Zedekiah's reign prior to Jeremiah's arrest. It is precisely at this seam in the narrative that once again we have reference to the scroll of 605 in the form of the narrative of its composition in chapter 36. In this fashion, chapters 26–35 are marked off as a second cycle of Jeremiah oracles.

Once again, chapters 37–44 move chronologically through the reign of Zedekiah in a third cycle of oracles and narratives until 46:1-2 forces another major retreat, this time back to the days of King Josiah. Once again, it is precisely at this juncture that we have reference made to the scroll written by Baruch in the fourth year of Jehoiakim (605 B.C.E.; 45:1).

It can hardly be accidental that every time the book of Jeremiah resets to an earlier historical period the next section is not only marked by a major rhetorical formula but is also directly preceded by a reference to the scroll of 605. This pattern of rhetoric, including the use of various forms of introductory formulae along with reference to the scroll of 605, divides the book of Jeremiah into three cycles of material. That the editor arranged the material in this fashion indicates the central role that this scroll was thought to have played in the book and in the ministry of Jeremiah. Whether Baruch is to be credited with such a major activity or it was the result of a longer process of Deuteronomistic editing, it seems clear how the book of Jeremiah presents itself to the reader to be read. It is not a haphazard collection of oracles defying logical ordering. It is, rather, a skillful literary compilation showing considerable artistic expertise, poetic beauty, and rhetorical sophistication.

CHAPTER 10

A Portrait
of the Prophet Jeremiah

From History to Literature

Due to increasing awareness of the Deuteronomistic editing of major sections of the Old Testament, including the book of Jeremiah, there has been a related move away from focusing on the person of Jeremiah to focusing instead on the structure, form, and significance of the book itself. This move is part of a contemporary concern in hermeneutics to shift from a historical-critical to a literary-critical study of Scripture. It is generally admitted today that the ability to describe history with adequate objectivity is compromised; it is at best extremely difficult and at worst impossible and illusory. The sources are often considered so tendentious and driven by ideological or partisan commitments that the data lying behind the sources are impossible to capture in any meaningful way. If history is impossible to define or capture, then we must turn to the study of the sources themselves—not for what they can tell us about their subject matter but rather for what they can tell us about the communities who produced them or the readers who subsequently have read them. Or we read the text for no other reason than to focus on its own literary integrity as a piece of art, an artifact of meaning and even of faith in its own right.

This hermeneutical shift away from history to literature is an important corrective to the naïve optimism with which historians have sometimes worked. To recognize the integrity of the *text itself* is a great gain especially for biblical study and biblical theology. The text is not simply a body of evidence that is studied in order to capture a historical reality that lies behind the text—whether close at hand or shrouded by ideology. The text itself is worthy of study. The text *itself* is the "Word" of God in some sense.

Once having admitted this point, however, and taking it with full seriousness, the question has to be asked whether history has any capacity at all to bear meaning and truth. Why is it important, in other words, to consider the issue of a "historical Jeremiah" at all? Biblical theology itself insists that God invests the divine self precisely in creation, as the divinely spoken word brings about the materiality of the world (Genesis 1). God's will becomes known, we believe, in the particularity of human history—in Israel, in exile, in the promise of restoration—and communities of faith believe in primary moments of history: exodus, Moses, David, and Jesus of Nazareth. It is not so significant, Christians believe, that God became *human*. What is critical for the Christian community is the belief that this incarnation, this emptying out of the divine into human form, was manifest in pinpoint historical particularity in the person of Jesus of Nazareth, in his life, death, and resurrection. Biblical theology itself argues that it is insufficient to leave God as an abstract concept or a general literary artifact. God became flesh and was "born of a woman, born under the law," as Paul says (Gal 4:4). The primary moment of our faith is one marked by absolute historical particularity in which the divine subjects itself to the contingencies of human history.

To jettison history as though it had no capacity to bear meaning and truth would be to deny a central Christian belief that "the finite is capable of bearing the infinite." If biblical theology itself is committed to the principle that the finite possesses such power, that the particularities and contingencies of history bear God incarnate, then it is biblical theology itself that insists that history is not bankrupt. It is not simply the *book* of Jeremiah that bears meaning. The *person* of Jeremiah also becomes a locus for precisely that historical particularity and contingency to which we are committed.

What Sort of Portrait?

It is popular today to say that the book of Jeremiah gives us a portrait of the prophet. This language attempts to find middle ground between a naïve historicist view on one hand that takes the sources too literally, as though they were purely objective and capable of giving us a photograph of the prophet, and a suspicious and skeptical view on the other hand that insists that the sources are shaped by later interests intent on creating a misleading persona that leads us away from the historical figure of Jeremiah. Most contemporary commentators and scholars of Jeremiah find themselves toward the middle of this continuum. As such, the common view that the book of Jeremiah provides us with a portrait of Jeremiah expresses an optimism regarding our ability to trust the sources to a great extent.

To suggest that the book provides us with a portrait of the prophet is meaningful. It does not, however, tell us what sort of portrait this is. Is it like a portrait by Jan Vermeer, in which one can see every nuance of facial expression, every wrinkle and mole, as though one were looking into a mirror image of the subject? Is it like a portrait by Pieter Brueghel, which attempts to capture the energy of a person with comedic or ironic imagination? Or is it perhaps like a Picasso, where noses and eyes will show up in the strangest of places, where essence is more prized than realistic appearance? What *sort* of portrait of the prophet do we have?

Scholars range widely on this issue. My concern is to take seriously what the book can tell us about the person of Jeremiah unless we find evidence to call the text into question. In this regard I would place myself more toward the Vermeer end of the spectrum than the Picasso, though I recognize the dangers of being naïve about such matters. I do not believe that the text intentionally seeks to lead us away from the person of Jeremiah toward a fictional persona. It may, at times, *unintentionally* do so, and we need to be critical of the text in order to sense those moments.

Jeremiah among the Priests

According to 1:1, Jeremiah was "from the priests who were in Anathoth." Though this note is vague, it raises an intriguing possibility.

Anathoth was the town, north of Jerusalem in the old tribal holding of Benjamin, to which the priest Abiathar had been exiled by King Solomon several hundred years before Jeremiah's time (1 Kgs 2:26-27). This exile of Abiathar to Anathoth was part of a larger political purge in which Solomon, who had just taken over the throne of his father David, was now attempting to consolidate control over his adversaries. Solomon had been opposed by representatives of an "old guard" establishment comprised of leaders who supported the old tribal alliances and traditions. The leaders of this old guard were Joab, the general of Israel's militia, and the priest Abiathar, who had been with David from his early days in the Negev and at Hebron. Joab and Abiathar lined up behind David's son Adonijah, born at Hebron and representing non-Jerusalemite interests. The "new guard" comprised those who represented David's newly found commitment to Jerusalem and to the development of a Jerusalemite ideology independent of the old tribal alliances and traditions. Leading this new guard were Benaiah, the general of David's personal troops; Nathan, the court prophet of David; and the priest Zadok, who was likely a former priest of the Jebusite (Jerusalemite) cult of El Elyon, that is, "Most High God," the deity worshiped in Jebus prior to David's conquest (Gen 14:18-20; Deut 32:8). This Zadok was maintained by David to foster a continuity with the Jerusalemite traditions. Benaiah, Nathan, and Zadok lined up in support of David's younger son, Solomon, who was born in Jerusalem and whose very name reflected the Jerusalemite tradition (Salem). Also in support of Solomon was David's favorite wife, Bathsheba, who happened to be Solomon's mother. It was Solomon who won the contest for David's throne, with the result that his adversaries were eventually killed or dispatched to exile. In this purge Abiathar, who had the misfortune of supporting the losing claimant to the throne, was exiled to Anathoth.

As one of the "priests from Anathoth," Jeremiah may well have been descended from these disenfranchised priests who had been cut off from temple service in the Jerusalem sanctuary. If so, one can easily imagine the sort of burning resentment that would have shaped their attitude toward the Zadokite establishment that controlled the temple cult. One can also imagine the importance of their collective memory, which recalled the fate suffered by their ancient and venerable ancestral sanctuary at Shiloh early in Israel's history during the days of their ancestor Eli (cf. 1 Sam 4:1-17). This recollection of

Shiloh's destruction lies behind Jeremiah's words of warning that, in spite of the people's naïve optimism, the temple in Jerusalem would fare no better than did the sanctuary at Shiloh (Jer 7:12-14; 26:6).

If this "Abiatharite" background of Jeremiah is fairly reliable, then specific information about strained and contentious relationships with his family members is less reliable. It is often assumed that members of his own family resisted Jeremiah for some reason, and that they tried to undermine his actions and even sought his harm. There is, however, scant evidence for such an inner-family conflict. The reference in 11:21 to threatening opposition by "the men of Anathoth" may indicate that Jeremiah had angered the general population of his hometown (cf. the reference to Jeremiah's "familiar friends" in 20:10). However, the text may as likely be a literary device linking this threat against Anathoth (that is, "City of Answers") to the context, in which Jeremiah is commanded not to pray for the towns of Judah (Jer 11:14), not to intercede on their behalf to secure divine oracles for their comfort. Even the city that prides itself on answers to such inquiries will receive no answer, and God will no longer listen (11:11).

The only reference specifically to Jeremiah being opposed by members of his own family is the statement in 12:6 that "even your brothers and the house of your father" have dealt treacherously with Jeremiah. The reference to such familial treachery, however, is certainly a literary device that prepares for the divine statement in the next verse: "I have forsaken my house, I have abandoned my heritage" (note the occurrence of the word "heritage" twice more in vv. 8-9). God's abandonment of the "house" (*bet*) of Israel is symbolized by Jeremiah's fractured relationship with the "house" (*bet*) of his father.

That Jeremiah faced social opposition is certain. However, this is one part of a developed persona that the editorial process attempted to enhance. In this process a number of complaint psalms are ascribed to Jeremiah, often referred to as "the confessions of Jeremiah" (11:18-20; 12:1-4; 15:15-18; 17:14-18; 18:19-23; 20:7-18). But such psalms of complaint are so stylized that they were likely drawn from a traditional stock of such psalms and placed in the mouth of Jeremiah by the editor to enhance Jeremiah's persona as the "suffering prophet." It is difficult to see in these psalms much more than an editorializing of the material to add a particular dimension to the prophet's character. This is not to deny that Jeremiah had real confrontations with community leaders, as we will see. It is to suggest, however, that the language of opposition by those even most intimately connected to him is part of the brushstrokes added by later editorial retouching.

Jeremiah among the Prophets

Even though Jeremiah was from priestly ancestry, he clearly understood himself to be a prophet. Unlike Amos and others, he does not deny his calling. According to the Jeremiah tradition, Jeremiah resisted his initial call with concern that he was only "a youth" (Hebrew *na'ar*; Jer 1:6). The term indicates not only age but also, more importantly, professional status, and the term likely meant that Jeremiah understood himself to be insufficiently trained for such a task. He thought of himself as a mere rookie, an apprentice. But such resistance is itself part of the prophetic tradition, and it would only be anticipated in the literary development of the tradition that the one so called would initially resist. That is what genuine prophets did!

Jeremiah used the "language" of a prophet and he engaged in the symbolic actions of a prophet. Indeed, no prophet besides Ezekiel gives us a clearer picture of *how* it was that prophets behaved socially. Wearing and then discarding a linen loincloth to symbolize God making the people "cling" to God but yet being "spoiled" (13:1-11); self-deprivation as a sign, in this case not taking a wife (16:1-4); the purchase and breaking of a clay juglet (*baqbuk*) as a symbol of God "emptying out" (*baqaq*) the plans of Judah and Jerusalem (19:1-13); wearing a yoke as a sign of Judah being yoked in Babylonian servitude (27:1—28:17); redeeming family property as a sign that "fields would again be bought and deeds signed, sealed, and witnessed" one day (32:6-44); the burying of stones in Egypt as a sign of Babylonian victory (43:8-13); and the throwing of a scroll into the Euphrates River as a sign that Babylon shall sink (51:59-64). Such a proliferation of prophetic sign-actions helps us understand how Jeremiah identified himself professionally as a prophet.

If Jeremiah understood himself to be a prophet in Judah, he also understood himself to be locked in a battle against false prophets for the hearts of the people. The term "false prophet" is never used apart from the Greek translation, which sometimes uses the term *pseudoprophetes* to describe these opponents. The Hebrew refers to them as "prophets who prophesy a lie" to the people. The lie is that everything will be all right, that peace will prevail (e.g., 14:13-16). The prime illustration of this prophetic lie is the account of Jeremiah's confrontation with the prophet Hananiah, related in 28:1-17. Hananiah's optimistic promise is that within two years the political disaster will reverse itself, and the temple vessels and Jerusalem leaders will come home from exile. Jeremiah counters this prophecy of peace by citing prophetic tradition and insisting that any prophet who prophesies peace must bear the burden of proof (28:8-9). Such prophets carelessly say "Peace! Peace!" when there is no peace, and in so doing they are simply smearing useless salve on the nation's mortal wound (6:14; 8:11; 14:13).

Jeremiah and the Jerusalem Leadership

Jeremiah had mixed relationships with the various kings of Judah during whose reigns he conducted his prophetic ministry. We saw before that Jeremiah probably began his career already during the early years of the Josianic reform movement and undoubtedly supported Josiah, becoming allies with the reform-minded family of Shaphan, Josiah's secretary. But after Josiah's death in 609 B.C.E., the reform probably lapsed and Jeremiah began a new phase in his ministry. How Jeremiah felt about Shallum, Josiah's immediate successor, is difficult to tell, since Shallum reigned only three months. The only indication we have is the comment made in 22:10-12, suggesting that Jeremiah considered Shallum an object of pity to be mourned: "Do not weep for him who is dead [Josiah], nor bemoan him; weep rather for him who goes away, for he shall return no more to see his native land."

Jeremiah's relationship with Jehoiakim, however, was bitter and contentious, and it was during these years (609–597 B.C.E.) that Jeremiah was tried publicly (26:1-24, dated to the beginning of Jehoiakim's reign, ca. 609), was later punished by being beaten and placed in the stocks (20:1-2, an oracle placed last in the group of oracles relating to King Jehoiakim in the first cycle of oracles), and was subsequently banned from the temple (36:5). That Jeremiah's relationship with Jehoiakim was bitter is exemplified in the "warm reception" that the king gives to Jeremiah's scroll when he burns it in the fire pit (36:23). Whereas Josiah was a model of justice, his son Jehoiakim was a symbol of perverse injustice and cruelty, and no one would mourn for him after his humiliating death and burial (22:13-19).

As with Shallum, Jeremiah's relationship with Jehoiachin was too brief to provide a clear picture of their interaction. He too appears to be an object of pity for Jeremiah. Carried into exile after only a few months on the throne, he was "a despised broken pot" hurled into an unknown land, to be written off as childless because he would provide no heir to the throne. In fact, Jehoiachin appears to have been the object of considerable hope for the exiled community, in whom there were messianic aspirations. Jeremiah, like many around him, considered the community that had been exiled to Babylon to be Judah's future hope, its "good figs" (24:1-7), and Jehoiachin, though in exile, was generally regarded as Judah's real king in whom Judean hopes continued to reside in spite of the fact that his uncle Zedekiah was on the throne in Jerusalem.

Jeremiah's relationship with Zedekiah, the last king of Judah, was mixed. He was, in the end, the "king of the bad figs," those left in the land after the first deportation (24:8-10). Zedekiah appears to have been too weak-willed to exert royal authority in the face of the final Babylonian crisis. The texts suggest that, while Zedekiah wanted to give Jeremiah intense regard and even follow his advice to capitulate to the Babylonians, he had lost control of the real tools of authority, and powerful princely families were pushing for resistance and sustained revolt. Zedekiah took pains to approach Jeremiah for intercession, advice, and counsel (37:3, 16-17; 38:14), but he was helpless before his strong advisors. Zedekiah appears to have wanted to help Jeremiah in whatever way he could, such as easing his final confinement in the court of the guard (37:20-21). But Zedekiah was paralyzed by his impotence in the face of his royal officials (38:5) and by his fear of being abused and killed by Jews who had already defected (38:19). It was during the final days of the Babylonian siege that Jeremiah was arrested on charges that he was leaving the city in order to desert to the Babylonians (37:11-15). In fact, he had simply been on his way to his hometown of Anathoth in order to take care of some family-related business. But these charges of desertion landed him in prison, where he spent the final days until Jerusalem fell to the Babylonians.

The royal officials, however, were not all opposed to Jeremiah. The story of Jeremiah's arrest in 609 B.C.E. suggests that, at this early date, these officials (Hebrew *sarim*, perhaps "princes") were cautious and

not willing to prosecute Jeremiah (26:16). As the position of the officials hardened, however, their ranks were apparently split over basic
matters of foreign policy. As we saw earlier, Jeremiah had strong sup-
porters among the princes. The family of Shaphan was a major political ally of Jeremiah and undoubtedly provided a security net for him.
How the royal officials were divided on the matter of capitulation to
the Babylonians is impossible to tell, though the pro-surrender party
was undoubtedly smaller than the pro-war party. We have an intriguing glimpse of this palace dispute recorded in the Lachish Letters,
texts found at the Judean city of Lachish and dating to the final days
of the Babylonian siege. In one of these letters an army general com-
plains that some of the princes are "weakening the hands" of his
troops, that is, impairing their morale to sustain the resistance under
siege conditions. One cannot read these painful complaints without
thinking of the royal family of Shaphan, wondering if perhaps it was
Ahikam, Gemariah, or Gedaliah whom the author of this text had in
mind.

The Deferral of Peace

Jeremiah had an unusually stormy career. Unlike the situation with
Isaiah, there appears to have been no major breaks during which
Jeremiah could recover. Even the fall of Jerusalem did not end his
career. While we might wish that the final years of Jeremiah had been
spent peacefully tending a garden in Anathoth, the last we see of Jeremiah is as he is being taken hostage with Jews fleeing to Egypt. His
last oracles are as bitter and devastating as his first (42:15-22; 43:8-13;
44:1-14, 20-30). "Behold, I am watching over them (*shoqed*) for evil
and not for good" (44:27). The final word of the book recalls Jeremiah's initial oracle. Jeremiah's first vision, that of a stick from an
almond tree (*shaqed*), was a sign that God was "watching over"
(*shoqed*) his word of judgment to perform it (1:11-12). The end of the
book comes full circle. We might wish that it were otherwise, but
sometimes it cannot be. God's word of judgment must be allowed to
achieve its goal, and we cannot hurry it in a rush to gospel and salvation. Jeremiah is a living example that sometimes the vision of peace
must be deferred even beyond the grave.

CHAPTER 11

Plucking Up
and Tearing Down

◆

The International Context
of Jeremiah's Judgment Oracles

The vast majority of Jeremiah's prophetic oracles were focused directly on the leadership and the people of Judah and Jerusalem. Nevertheless, we saw earlier that it was not at all uncommon for prophets also to be attributed oracles against the nations, as was the case with Amos and Isaiah of Jerusalem. Jeremiah too had a lengthy collection of such oracles attributed to him, directed against Egypt, Philistia, Moab, Ammon, Edom, Aram, Babylon, and other nations in western Asia. Beyond these oracles, however, the message of Jeremiah was intentionally placed within an international context in several ways: Jeremiah envisions Judah and Jerusalem as being swept up in international events as nations from the "north" are unleashed upon the entire world (e.g., 4:6; 6:1, 22; 10:22). From the very first oracle, Jeremiah's oracles against Judah are placed within the context of a boiling pot that is spilling over from the north (1:13-16). As was mentioned earlier, the concept of the "north" was part of the mythical conception of the world. Just as Babylon would be Judah's "foe from the north" (25:8-26), so Babylon too would meet its own "foe from the north" that would eventually crush it (50:9).

Whether it was part of the prophet's own self-understanding or part of the prophet's persona enhanced by the Deuteronomistic editing, the book presents Jeremiah's oracles as set within a context in which Jeremiah is not simply sent to Judah and Jerusalem but is appointed as a "prophet to the nations," set over them for the twofold task of uprooting and then of planting, of tearing down and then of building up (1:5-10). This twofold prophetic commission gives the book its energy, as it moves between these two poles with words of judgment and of restoration. God is not engaged simply in domestic remodeling. This divine drama involves a cosmos-wide reconstruction program.

Israel's Pristine Holiness

Taking up the theme characteristic of Deuteronomic theology and already developed in the book of Hosea, Jeremiah understood Israel's problem to center on its attraction to the fertility cult characteristic of indigenous Canaanite religion. Prior to their encounter with the "land of grain, wine, and oil," the people enjoyed a pristine relationship with God in which Israel's residency in the wilderness was regarded as a honeymoon period (Jer 2:1-3). The "devotion of Israel's youth" made Israel the cherished delight of God—belonging intimately to God in the same way as did the sacrifices offered by the priests that were "holy to the Lord." But just as these holy sacrifices were off-limits to profane consumption, and anyone who illegitimately ate of them became guilty ('asham) before God (Lev 22:10-16), so Israel's enemies became guilty ('asham) whenever they attempted to consume Israel (Jer 2:3).

In spite of this holy intimacy and protection, however, Israel abandoned Yahweh's love and devotion. The chief sign of this abandonment was that, after a while, Israel stopped complaining to God (Jer 2:4-8). The shocking development is not that Israel refused to love a God who performed such marvelous acts on Israel's behalf as deliverance from Egypt, guidance in the wilderness, and leading them into the land of promise. The shocking development, rather, is that they ceased *complaining*. They ceased saying "Where is the Lord!" ('ayyeh YHWH, 2:6, 8). This exclamation is precisely drawn from the language of Israel's complaint psalms, of religious taunting, when the psalmist in his frustration and feeling of God-forsakenness asks "Where is God?!" (Ps 42:3, 10; 79:10; 115:2; Isa 36:19; Job 35:10). God invited Israel's complaints. God craved Israel's challenges for the divine to rise to its crises. When the people ceased complaining to God or challenging God, that loss of intimacy was the sign that Israel no longer cared enough to remain "holy to the Lord."

God would not easily give up on Israel, however. One of the unique themes of the book of Jeremiah is its view of the prophets. On many occasions, as we shall see, Jeremiah vehemently criticizes "the prophets" who prophesy lying visions of their own minds. It confronts us as one of the book's many tensions, therefore, when the book also stresses that the prophets were "God's servants" who had been sent by God to warn the people to turn from their evil ways. This theme is a hallmark of Deuteronomistic historiography, one of the major convictions of the Deuteronomistic Historian (e.g., 2 Kgs 17:13, 23; 21:10; 24:2). Jeremiah utilizes this same theme, but emphasizes the divine intentionality by stressing the persistence with which God sent these prophetic servants. Over and over, Jeremiah stresses that God *"persistently* sent his servants the prophets" to the people, only to have them rejected and abused (Jer 7:25; 25:4; 26:5; 29:19; 35:15; 44:4). This theme of divine persistence is marked by the use of the peculiar grammatical construction joining a finite verb with two infinitive absolutes, including the infinitive *hashkem*, "starting early" (Jer 7:13; 11:7; 25:3; 32:33; 35:14). God "sent persistently," God "spoke persistently," God "taught persistently." This persistence in sending the prophets was only one aspect of the broader pattern of divine persistence in general. No one stresses this divine persistence as does Jeremiah, for whom the theme approaches canonical status. God would not easily give up on Israel, his "holy delight."

Baal—the Big Lie

The enchantment of Canaanite religion was, in this Deuteronomistic view, too powerful for Israel to resist. This Canaanite cult was expressed through a devotion to a number of different gods who were related to one another as a "family" or a closely knit community: El, the high god; Asherah, the divine "mother"; Ishtar, the "queen of heaven"; Mot and Yam, the dangerous gods of "death" and "chaotic sea," respectively. In addition, other national deities had been introduced into the system, such as Chemosh, the god of the Moabites, and Milcom (perhaps also referred to as Molech), the god of the Ammonites. The chief symbol of this entire system, however, was the heroic god of fertility, storm, and seasonal rains—Baal. The name "Baal" stood *pars pro toto* for the cultic system of indigenous Canaanite worship and belief.

Israel's apostasy was demonstrated by the charge that its prophets "prophesied by Baal" (2:8) and the nation had "changed its glory for that which does not profit," a satirical play on the words *ba'al* ("Baal") and *wa'al* ("avail," "profit," "benefit"; cf. 7:8; 12:13; 16:19). Baal does not avail. Baal cannot guarantee rain and fertility, but rather is like a broken cistern that leaks out its illusory hopes (2:13). Baal and other gods will not be able to save when the day of crisis comes, no matter how earnestly the people appeal to them for deliverance (11:9-13). Jeremiah castigates apostate rituals such as those of burning children as sacrificial offerings to Baal that took place at Topheth in the Valley of Hinnom, just south of the city (19:1-6). Baal was "that *shameful* thing" that devoured everything for which Israel's ancestors had worked (3:24). Indeed, a common literary device in Deuteronomistically influenced writings was to refer to Baal as "shame" (*boshet*), even substituting the vowels of the word *boshet* for words that the author wished to disparage, as when the name Merib-baal (1 Chr 8:34; 9:40) is rendered by the Deuteronomistic Historian as Mephiboshet (2 Sam 9:6-13; cf. the Deuteronomistic Historian's use of the name *'ishboshet*, 2 Sam 2:8-15). Baal was indeed the "shame of Israel." Like Isaiah before him, Jeremiah engaged in a typical form of mockery of the idolatry that was a part of Canaanite worship; mere pieces of wood, hammered silver and gold, unmovable like "scarecrows in a cucumber field" (10:3-5).

In its lust for material affluence and fertility that it thought could be guaranteed by these Canaanite gods, Israel acted shamelessly, like a wild donkey in heat sniffing the wind, like a lost and loose camel chasing helter-skelter in circles (2:20-25), like oversexed stallions neighing over the filly next door (5:7-8). Israel was like the proverbial "lady in red," all rouged, bejeweled, and ready for action, destined to be disappointed by lovers who cared nothing for her and meant her only harm (4:30). In this hormone-driven quest for gratification, Israel was so confused that she could not even keep her apostasy straight. Confusing the symbols of Baal (*massebah*, "stone pillar," 2 Kgs 3:2) and Asherah (*'asherah*, "sacred wood pole," 1 Kgs 16:33), the people "say to a tree, 'You are my father,' and to a stone, 'You gave me birth'" (Jer 2:27). They could not even keep their apostate iconography in order. They could not tell "mommy" from "daddy"! But Israel's affection for these cultic practices was overpowering, and Israel would never give them up. When the crisis finally hit with full force, the people of Judah put an uncanny spin on the matter, arguing that it was precisely because Josiah had forced Judah to put aside its idolatry and apostasy that the disaster had fallen on them. Back when they engaged in "baking cakes for the queen of heaven," everything had been wonderful. They had no intention of giving up these practices for what they understood to be the self-defeating interests of worshiping Yahweh alone (7:18; 44:15-19)!

On one hand, then, Israel's chief problem was its religious apostasy, its abandonment of Yahweh, the fountain of living water, in order to dig out cracked cisterns for Baal's rains. But the problem was not that simple. More than likely there was a serious blurring of distinctions between the benefits and actions of Yahweh and those of Baal and the other deities of the land. In all likelihood, the people could not make a neat distinction between worshiping Yahweh and worshiping Baal. They most likely were fusing attributes and characteristics of the various gods together so much that they did not know where Yahweh left off and Baal began, or how it was that Yahweh differed from Baal in the first place. After all, if the word *ba'al* was a social designation meaning "husband," "master," "owner," then could not Yahweh *be* Israel's Baal? We earlier saw how this confusion between Yahweh and Baal was expressed in the famous words of Hosea: "On that day, says the Lord, you will call me, 'My husband,' and no longer will you call me, 'My Baal'" (Hos 2:16). After all, twice we read in the book of Jeremiah itself that God had intentionally "become *ba'al*" to Israel (Jer 3:14, *ki 'anoki ba'alti bakem*; Jer 31:32, *we'anoki ba'alti bam*). These are shocking words whose punch is lost in the usual translations. God had "Baaled" himself to Israel. That the verb *ba'al* could possibly be used to define God's relationship with Israel helps us understand the sort of confusion that must have existed in popular minds, the sort of confusion that would lie behind the note in Hosea 2:16—someday the people will stop referring to Yahweh as "Baal."

This blurring of the distinction between Yahweh and Baal, this confusion over whether Yahweh *was* in fact Baal, can be seen in texts such as Jeremiah 23:26-32. Just as Israel's ancestors had forgotten Yahweh's name for that of Baal, so Jeremiah's adversaries are causing Israel to forget Yahweh's name by their lying dreams. But it is not that these prophets are actually prophesying in the name of Baal. The text is clear that these prophets are indeed prophesying in the very name of Yahweh (v. 31). We should not assume, then, that Jeremiah's adversaries were clear heretics who believed in Baal rather than in Yahweh and who clearly prophesied in the very name of Baal. In all likelihood, these prophets claimed the name of Yahweh and claimed to be speaking in his name. But they may so have confused the social title of *ba'al* with the identity of Yahweh that it led to a perversion of what Yahweh represented.

The Other Lie: False Confidence in God

It is far from clear, then, what it means that Jeremiah accused the prophets of prophesying in the name of Baal. These prophets were likely prophesying using the name of Yahweh. What they were prophesying in Yahweh's name, however, tells the tale. The lie that these prophets were prophesying was the promise that everything would be all right, that Yahweh would protect the people, that nothing bad would happen to them, that they were secure in their self-absorbed narcissism. The prophets were promising salvation in the very name of Yahweh, predicting peace where there clearly was no peace and when destruction was at the doorstep. They were healing the nation's wound with ineffective salve and unsterile bandages (6:14; 8:11; 14:13-16). None of them had truly stood in the council of the Lord, and Yahweh sent none of them (23:16-22).

Such an astounding and shocking false sense of security was delusional. Even the temple itself had become the chief symbol of this corporate delusion. The people could come fresh from their latest criminal treachery, their hands stained with theft, murder, adultery, false oaths, and religious apostasy, and come to the temple invoking "sanctuary" as though it were a robbers' hideout. Here "we are safe!" (*nissalnu*, 7:8-11). They cannot touch us here!

So again we see in 7:8-9 that it is not possible to distinguish between matters of worshiping the right god and worshiping God rightly. The offensiveness of social injustice was one with that of an astounding religious presumptuousness that took Yahweh's love and comfort for granted. All of this is precisely what it meant to "worship other gods." To worship Baal did not mean simply to worship the god named Baal.

More importantly, it meant to worship Yahweh as though he *were* Baal, as though he functioned as *ba'al* to Israel: owner, master, lord, guarantor of all material well-being, sugar daddy. No matter what Israel did, no matter how offensive its social injustice, how murderous its oppression, Yahweh would take care of it, so the people thought. Their sugar daddy would slather well-being and security on them and see that everything was all right.

This collision of basic religious convictions was most dramatically seen in Jeremiah's confrontation with the prophet Hananiah. Humans have an uncanny ability to continue believing in the impossible, to continue insisting that a cherished conviction is true even when it has been disproved by one body of evidence after another. Psychologists refer to this as "cognitive dissonance," the ability to continue believing in something ("cognition") even when it is "dissonant" with the realities with which we are faced. Hananiah's ability to continue promising peace in the wake of the first deportation and continued Babylonian control was truly astounding, a remarkable example of cognitive dissonance.

Jeremiah understood Israel's offense to be utterly incomprehensible. Characteristic once again of a Deuteronomic view of life, Israel should easily have known better. After all, the law is not in heaven so high that it is scarcely fathomable or over the seas so far that it can scarcely be reached. It is in your mouth and in your heart, and it is not too hard for you (Deut 30:11-14). So Jeremiah stresses the utter unnaturalness of Israel's disobedience. No nation ever changes its gods, but Israel did (Jer 2:10-11). Brides do not forget their attire, but Israel forgot God (2:32). People who fall get up again; people who get lost turn around, but not Israel (8:4-5). The birds know when to come and go with the seasons, but Israel does not have a clue about God's ordinances (8:7). Snow and water never leave the mountains, but Israel left God (18:14-15). Yet the people claim to be wise (*hakam*). Given these circumstances, God suggests that the only one who is wise is the one who has become skilled (*hakam*) in funeral dirges (8:8; 9:12-24). The requiem is the repository of all of Israel's wisdom.

The Irrevocability of Judgment

Jeremiah's message was in many ways Israel's requiem. Judgment was irrevocable and doom was certain. Appeals for repentance in chapters

1–6 conclude with the language of the refiner's blast furnace in which Israel is to be refined: "The bellows blow fiercely, the lead is consumed by the fire; in vain the refining goes on, for the wicked are not removed. Refuse silver they are called, for the Lord has rejected them" (6:29-30).

The irrevocability of this judgment was sealed by the fact that Jeremiah was commanded by God not to intercede on Israel's behalf. Just as Isaiah had been commanded to ensure judgment in his era by "dulling their minds, stopping their ears, and shutting their eyes" (Isa 6:10), so Jeremiah was to ensure God's judgment by refusing intercession on their behalf (Jer 7:16). Neither such intercession nor fasting nor sacrificial offerings would stave off the sword, famine, and pestilence (14:11-12). Indeed, even if the two most renowned intercessors in Israel's corporate memory, Moses and Samuel, interceded on their behalf, it would be no use (15:1-2).

Judgment was irrevocable and inescapable. It would seem to the people as though Yahweh himself was fighting against Judah on behalf of the Babylonian army (21:3-6). It was Israel's own God who could be seen leading the Babylonians into battle against Jerusalem. Any people who survived the sword, famine, and pestilence might be tempted to consider themselves lucky. They should not be so presumptuous, however, as any survivors would simply be given into the hands of the Babylonians, who would "smite them with the edge of the sword; he shall not pity them, or spare them, or have compassion" (21:7).

Insisting strenuously on the irrevocability and inescapability of Judah's pending destruction, Jeremiah became known publicly as "Mr. Doom and Gloom." One of the central phrases in the book, which echoes throughout its pages, is "Terror is all around!" (*magor missabib*, e.g., 6:25; 46:5; 49:29). This is the nickname that Jeremiah gives to the priest Pashhur after Pashhur has him beaten, confined, and then banished from the temple (20:3-4). It is also the nickname that Jeremiah's adversaries use when taunting him. "Let us put an end to old Mr. Doom and Gloom!" (20:10). Jeremiah was convinced that nothing could now stave the tide of international events that had been set into motion: "Look, the storm of the Lord! Wrath has gone forth, a whirling tempest; it will burst upon the head of the wicked. The anger of the Lord will not turn back until he has executed and accomplished the intents of his mind. In the latter days you will understand it clearly" (23:19-20). But if the tide was inexorably rolling toward

Israel's shores, a sea of change was also welling up in its backwash. Jeremiah is the one prophet who straddled Judah's crisis of exile, and his word of judgment, of doom and gloom, was about to take a radical turn. Jeremiah's task of plucking up and breaking down was nearing its completion, and the second phase of his career awaited him. It would soon be time to "build and plant."

CHAPTER 12

Building and Planting: Looking to the Future

The Turn of the Tide

From the earliest point of Jeremiah's commission, his task was twofold: "See, today I appoint you over nations and over kingdoms, to pluck up and to pull down, to destroy and to overthrow, to build and to plant" (Jer 1:10). This language of uprooting and planting, of demolition and building, echoes throughout the pages of the book to remind the reader that the two are insolubly connected. Neither exists for its own sake nor without the other. God's terrible deeds of demolition must move forward. As Jeremiah stated to Baruch in the pivotal year of the commissioning of the first scroll: God would break down what he had built, and pluck up what he had planted (45:4). The episode involving the Rechabites in chapter 35 was a sign of Israel's pending destruction. Jeremiah was instructed to gather the clan of the Rechabites into the temple and invite them to drink from pitchers of wine. They refused to drink, however, because their family ethos dictated that they were to live as nomadic tent dwellers on the edges of civilization. They could neither "build" nor "sow" nor "plant" (vv. 6-7). Even given such a strange communal ethos, they nevertheless were faithful. But Israel could not listen to their own ethos, and they were doomed to have their lavish buildings demolished and their sown fields ripped out. The lesson of the potter was that God reserved the right to destroy the ruined pot and begin again to refashion a new creation. God exercises the freedom to "pluck up and break down and destroy" that which God had "built and planted" (18:5-10).

But if the metaphor of the potter held out hope that repentance might be possible (18:8), Judah seemed incapable of it. God's powerful appeals for apostate Israel to repent fell on deaf ears. "Return, faithless Israel!" (*shubah meshubah yisra'el*, 3:12), for God yearns to exercise mercy, not anger. "Return, O faithless children!" (*shubah banim shobabim*, 3:14, 22), for it is Yahweh who is their *ba'al*, and he will lead them back to Zion and heal their faithlessness. Such appeals for repentance already mark God's fierce passion for restoration and reconciliation. But if the people's fascination for Baal was to no avail, so too were these appeals for Israel's contrition. God's act of demolition would proceed. The bulldozers and wrecking cranes came to life.

But the tide turned in the midst of Jeremiah's ministry, and as the sounds of demolition echoed ever more loudly through the streets of Jerusalem, Jeremiah began to sound the call to envision the new community that would emerge. If Jeremiah's words of judgment and destruction, of sword, famine, and pestilence were difficult and unbelievable for the people to hear in the midst of their narcissistic optimism, the words of new life emerging from the rubble of destruction were even harder to fathom. Following the destruction of Jerusalem, the people did not have the energy or hope to hear any promise for the future. They could only lament their doom and the fall of their city to the Babylonians (32:36, 43): "It is a waste, without human or beast!" (33:10). Jeremiah, too, expressed his own incredulous disbelief when instructed by God to redeem some family property. What earthly sense would an investment in real estate make when the land lay ruined by the Babylonian siege (32:16-25)? But Jeremiah's action, as ill-timed as it seemed, was a sign that fields would again someday be bought, deeds signed and sealed (32:15, 43-44), and the fortunes of the people and the land restored.

The hammering sounds of demolition were to be replaced with the joyous sounds of rebuilding. The sounds of "building and planting" would supplant those of "tearing down and destroying" (24:6; 31:28). Indeed, Jeremiah insisted, this building program should not wait until the people returned from their seventy years of exile. Already in their exile they should exercise this vision of the future while at the same time growing accustomed to the longevity of their stay in Babylon. In a letter that Jeremiah sent to the *golah* ("exile") community, he instructed them to "build houses, plant gardens," and "seek the welfare (*shalom*) of the city." Such actions of hope and "restoration of Judah's fortunes" were not to await some future moment when they would be logical. They were to commence *now*, even in the midst of exile itself.

Jeremiah's Confrontation with God

God's fierce passion for the restoration of Judah can be seen in what is one of the chief characteristics of the book of Jeremiah: its portrayal of human and divine pathos, a yearning that is flooded with tears of regret and anguish. The prophet is portrayed as one who is overcome with the anguish of having to bear God's anger for the people, the weariness of having to hold it in his very being (Jer 6:11), like a raging fire in his bones (20:9). The pain that Jeremiah feels, however, is also God's own pain, and one characteristic of the book of Jeremiah is that the personality of prophet and God coalesce so thoroughly that at times it is impossible to distinguish the pain of one from that of the other. Who is it that speaks in 4:19-22, for example? Is it Jeremiah who "writhes in anguish and pain"? Or is it God, who cannot bear the foolishness of God's people? This grief shared by God and prophet seems beyond healing, sickening and wounding the heart, crying out for a reservoir of tears to drown the grief (8:18—9:1).

The movement from demolition to rebuilding is portrayed in Jeremiah's very life, seen in the series of complaint psalms that are often referred to collectively as the "confessions of Jeremiah." The pain of demolition and of Jerusalem's God-forsakenness is heard in Jeremiah's own cries of dereliction as Jeremiah accuses God of being like a stranger to the land (14:9). The persona of Jeremiah with which the reader is presented is that of the faithful servant who has been deceived and abandoned. Jeremiah gave up earthly companionship and circles of normal friendship only to sit isolated because of God's oppressive hand that was filling him with embarrassing indignation. Jeremiah felt that if Baal was nothing but a cracked cistern, then certainly Yahweh was only a "deceitful brook, which could not be trusted" (*ḳemo 'aḳzab mayim lo' ne'emanu*, 15:15-18). Using a term drawn from the violence of rape and seduction (Exod 22:16; Deut

11:16; Judg 14:15; 16:5; Hos 2:14; Job 31:9), Jeremiah accuses God of having "deceived" him (*pittitani YHWH wa'eppat*), of having mugged him and humiliated him (20:7). Jeremiah can only curse the very day of his birth and wish that his birth had been aborted (20:14-18).

The point is not to presume that we can capture a real-life picture of the historical Jeremiah, making him the poster child for the developing concept of Israel's suffering prophets. The point, rather, is to understand the metaphorical power of this persona, who in his very bones rehearses not only the anguish of the people as their world is being deconstructed but also the anguish of God, who similarly is torn apart in grief. God knows that the destruction of Israel can lead in very real ways to the deconstruction of the idea of God itself. Israel's disappearance from history would lead to ultimate questions not only about God's ability to save, but also about the very nature and existence of God (Ps 42:3, 10; 79:10; 115:2). In Israel's demise God was grieving not only the loss of relationship but the real threat of the loss of God's very identity.

Forgetting the Past

In the midst of this catastrophic threat, God wagers not only the loss of divine identity but in fact the loss of Israel's entire collective memory. The demolition of Israel's identity is so radical that what lies in the future will fully swamp any attachment that Israel had to its rehearsal of sacred icons of the past. The chief icon of Israel's national status was the ark of the covenant, the very throne of God's glory. But the people are told that God's salvific purpose will make the memory of the ark itself a mere anachronism of history. "They shall no longer say, 'The ark of the covenant of the Lord.' It shall not come to mind, or be remembered, or missed; nor shall another one be made." Instead, Jerusalem itself shall be God's throne, and the memory of Israel's chief cultic icon of the past will become a meaningless anachronism (Jer 3:16-17).

Historical memory itself can easily become a community's chief icon. Just as the ark of the covenant would be forgotten, so too would Israel's cherished historical icons, its most prized historical memories of God's salvation. "Therefore, the days are surely coming, says the Lord, when it shall no longer be said, 'As the Lord lives who brought

the people of Israel up out of the land of Egypt. . . .'" Israel's constitutive event, the exodus itself, was an icon of Israel's past that would lose
its power to define the people, to anchor them in a past that had failed
them. Instead, they would look ahead and say, "As the Lord lives who
brought the people of Israel up out of the land of the north and out of
all the lands where he had driven them . . ." (16:14-15 = 23:7). Along
with the icons of Israel's cult and the icons of Israel's history itself, the
icons of Israel's excuses would also be excised from their memory.
"The days are surely coming, says the Lord. . . . In those days they
shall no longer say: 'The parents have eaten sour grapes, and the children's teeth are set on edge'" (31:27-29). Israel's excuses had become
part of its communal iconography. They were hung on their walls,
fixed in their courtyards, venerated and admired as though they were
protective talismans, magical charms that could ward off any threat or
disaster. But these icons too would be stripped from their walls and
relegated to the anachronisms of history. The icons of cult, of creed,
and of excuse would have no power to define the new creation that
was about to emerge.

A New Future

Like many in Judah during his days, Jeremiah apparently placed considerable hopes in the *golah* community, the "good figs" who would be
restored, built, and planted once again in the land (24:1-7). Scholars
assume that it was the exiled King Jehoiachin who, even in Babylonian captivity, continued to be regarded as the real king, in spite of the
fact that it was his uncle, Zedekiah, who was placed on the throne in
Jerusalem by the Babylonians. The continued importance of
Jehoiachin over his uncle is perhaps seen in the fact that a person
named Sheshbazzar is the leader of the *golah* community when they
return to Jerusalem, and this Sheshbazzar is referred to as "the prince
of Judah" (*nasi lihudah*, Ezra 1:2-11). Moreover, most believe that this
Sheshbazzar is identical to "Shenazzar," who is listed as the fourth
son of Jehoiachin in 1 Chronicles 3:18. In spite of Jeremiah's prophecy
that Jehoiachin was "as good as childless," having no heirs to follow
him on the throne (Jer 22:30), such may not have been the case. The
Deuteronomistic Historian certainly seems to hold out confidence
that Jehoiachin was Judah's hope for the future (2 Kgs 25:27-30), and

messianic hopes for a Davidic restoration may have attended Shesh-bazzar's leadership as Judah's prince.

Though the harboring of such messianic hopes may not have been characteristic of Jeremiah's own vision for Judah, the larger Jeremiah tradition certainly came to be imbued with such fervent hopes. A woe oracle addressed to Israel's kings (the "shepherds") in 23:1-4 gives way to the vision of "coming days" when a "righteous branch" (*semah tsad-diq*) would be raised up for the Davidic throne (23:5-6). If, as was mentioned above, Judah's messianic hopes were placed in the exiled King Jehoiachin, one can understand why Zedekiah serves here as the foil for what legitimate kingship is. This new king will have the title "Yahweh is our righteousness" (*YHWH tsidqenu*), an ironic play on the name Zedekiah (*tsidqiyahu*), meaning "Yahweh is my righteous-ness." The word "branch" becomes a standard title for Judah's mes-sianic hopes and is applied directly to Zerubbabel in Israel's postexilic reconstruction (Zech 3:8; 6:12), a branch that "shall execute justice and righteousness in the land" (Jer 23:5). In Jeremiah 33:14-18 a similar messianic hope is expressed in what is nearly an identical text. Here, however, the messianic hope is lodged less in the *person* of the king than in the *city* of Jerusalem itself. The focus of chapter 33 is on the cities of Judah and especially on Jerusalem throughout (vv. 4-5, 9, 10, 12-13). The chief difference between 23:6 and 33:16 is the pronoun referring to what it is that is named. In 23:6 the reference is to *his* name (*wezeh-shemo*), that is, the king. In 33:16, however, it is to *her* (*yiqra'-lah*), that is, to "the city." It might be, then, that 33:14-18 repre-sents an alternate hope in which Israel's messianic expectations are, in a sense, democratized and placed in the community as a whole, or politicized in the sense that it is the polis that comes to bear the hopes for Israel rather than the royal person.

The clearest and most sustained vision for Israel's restoration is in Jeremiah 30–33, sometimes referred to as "the Book of Consolation," but almost certainly made up of originally independent oracles in chapters 30–31 and a longer narrative in chapters 32–33. The basic rhetorical structure of the unit heightens anticipation of the "days that are coming" (*hinneh yamim ba'im*, 30:3; 31:27, 31, 38). The opening oracle—of God "watching over" Israel to bring destruction (1:11-12)—is reversed as now God promises to "watch over" them to build and to plant (31:28).

The promises of restoration reach their loudest crescendo with the promise of a "new covenant" in 31:31-34. This will not be like the old covenant, which God made with the people in becoming their *ba'al*, their guarantor of material well-being and security, their sugar daddy. What is new is not that this covenant will be written on their hearts. After all, the idea that the law was written on the human heart was a standard belief in terms of Deuteronomic theology (Deut 30:14). What is new, what is utterly shocking—given Jeremiah's grounding in Deuteronomic thought—is that this new covenant would not have to be taught. The enterprise of teaching was the basic social responsibility according to the book of Deuteronomy. Parents were to teach their children at every conceivable opportunity (Deut 4:10; 11:19). The law was to be passed down by teaching, from God to Moses to the people and to their children (Deut 5:31; 6:1). For Jeremiah to have a vision of the future in which there would be no teaching of the law must have stung the ears of everyone who heard it. The law would be so innately a part of the human condition that there would no longer be a need for teaching.

One final time Jeremiah calls upon the people to "turn," using the familiar word of repentance. "Return O virgin Israel!" (*shubi betulat yisra'el*, Jer 31:21). But this time the call is for Israel to return from its captivity, to return to its cities, "For the Lord has created a new thing on the earth: a woman protects a man." What this phrase means baffles and astounds scholars. What God's new promises entail similarly baffles and astounds all of God's people. The "Book of Consolation" gives us the longest sustained vision of restoration and promised peace in the writings of the preexilic prophets—one that baffles us by the mystery of God's grace and astounds us with its promise even while we cannot see beyond the rubble of our ruined city and our fractured past.

Daring to Glance Ahead

Jeremiah's prophetic career was anchored deeply in Israel's preexilic history and society, but he straddled the divide of exile that cut Israel's future off inexorably from its past. Jeremiah's call to forget the past would be taken up in even fuller tones by a prophet appearing in the circle of Isaiah, whom we refer to as Second Isaiah. This exilic prophet's call for the exiles to "not remember" Israel's broken past moved the community even more resolutely into the newness of its future (Isa 42:9; 43:18; 48:3-6; 54:4). While Israel was not to become enmeshed in its past, while it was not to be hobbled by the chains of anachronism, it is also clear that Israel could not simply move into the future with amnesia. Those who do not learn from the past are doomed to repeat it. So the same prophet likewise calls on Israel to remember its past (41:22; 46:9). All history came to be regarded as under the control of Yahweh, who declared what would be from the very beginning, even things not yet done (46:10). But it was the *new* thing that would reveal Yahweh's glory and desire, not the old thing revealed long ago. God's glory would be revealed in things heretofore unheard of, unimagined, unbelievable (48:6-7).

The experience of exile substantially reshaped the basic presuppositions of Israel's convictions about God, about the world, about history, and about its relationship with God. Preexilic theology tended to stress the contractual nature of covenant relationship, particularly canonized in Deuteronomic and Deuteronomistic theology. The exile was so catastrophic, however, that no longer could an understanding of God's love for Israel be predicated solely on the idea of a contract in which there were mutual obligations. Already in Jeremiah we have a dramatic shift to language concerning the irrevocable and permanent nature of the relationship from henceforth. God's commitment to the people is as firmly fixed as are the orders of the universe itself, and only when the stars fall from their places in heaven or day and night decide to change places with one another will anything change between God and the people (Jer 31:35-37; 33:19-26).

This shift from a contractual understanding of covenant to one that stresses the permanence and eternity of divine commitment to Israel becomes a hallmark of the postexilic Priestly tradition, as it adopted the technical term *berit 'olam* ("eternal covenant") to define this relationship. In its own way, Priestly theology came to stress the absolutely fundamental centrality of God's grace in the life of the people—a grace that overcame the fact that never had there been even a day of obedience on Israel's part, and never could God count on Israel's ability or desire to repent (e.g., Ezekiel 20). Relationship had nothing to do with Israel's fidelity or repentance, but everything to do with God's commitment to the integrity of what it meant to be "God."

Postexilic prophecy is not, however, a radically new phenomenon, cut off from its preexilic roots by some unbridgeable chasm. Ezekiel, Second Isaiah, Third Isaiah, Haggai, Zechariah, and Malachi all pursue traditions laid down by their preexilic forebears and understand themselves to stand in a long prophetic tradition. But with Zechariah and the night visions that he reports (Zechariah 1–8), we have the gradual shift into a form of literature that has different purposes than did literary prophecy. "Apocalyptic" literature evolved from literary prophecy, but its concern was less to provide a theological and social commentary on current issues than to bolster the confidence of the faithful that history had always been and continues to be in God's controlling hands. Literary prophecy was preaching to the disobedient and unrepentant, urging them toward a conversion over which God had little final control. Apocalyptic, in this sense, was preaching to the choir, giving them confidence that, if they were aware of the secrets of history, they could see that everything was unfolding just as God had intended from the very beginning. These themes of divine control were only in their nascent state in preexilic prophecy. The exile, however, was a major watershed in this regard. The chaos of Judah's destruction was so unsettling that the notion of a history left open to the human will to decide regarding matters of life and death (Jer 21:8) was painful and frightening. Apocalyptic literature came to overcome this painful and frightening openness and ambiguity of history.

Select Bibliography
on Prophecy

Balentine, Samuel E. "The Prophet as Intercessor: A Reassessment." *Journal of Biblical Literature* 103 (1984) 161–73.

Baltzer, Klaus. "Considerations regarding the Office and Calling of the Prophet." *Harvard Theological Review* 61 (1968) 567–81.

———. *Deutero-Isaiah: A Commentary on Isaiah 40–55.* Translated by Margaret Kohl. Hermeneia. Minneapolis: Fortress Press, 2001.

Ben Zvi, Ehud, and Michael H. Floyd, editors. *Writings and Speech in Israelite and Ancient Near Eastern Prophecy.* Society of Biblical Literature Symposium Series 10. Atlanta: Scholars Press, 2000.

Blenkinsopp, Joseph. *A History of Prophecy in Israel.* Rev. ed. Louisville: Westminster John Knox, 1996.

Brennemann, James E. *Canons in Conflict: Negotiating Texts in True and False Prophecy.* New York: Oxford Univ. Press, 1997.

Bright, John. *Covenant and Promise: The Prophetic Understanding of the Future in Pre-exilic Israel.* Philadelphia: Westminster, 1976.

Brueggemann, Walter. *Hopeful Imagination: Prophetic Voices in Exile.* Philadelphia: Fortress Press, 1986.

———. *The Prophetic Imagination.* 2d ed. Minneapolis: Fortress Press, 2001.

———. *Texts That Linger, Words That Explode: Listening to Prophetic Voices.* Edited by Patrick D. Miller. Minneapolis: Fortress Press, 2000.

Carroll, Robert P. "Prophecy and Society." In *The World of Ancient Israel*. Edited by R. E. Clements, 203–25. Cambridge: Cambridge Univ. Press, 1989.

Chaney, Marvin L. "Bitter Bounty: The Dynamics of Political Economy Critiqued by the Eighth-Century Prophets." In *Reformed Faith and Economics*. Edited by Robert L. Stivers, 15–30. Lanham, Md.: University Press of America, 1989.

Clements, Ronald E. "Patterns in the Prophetic Canon." In *Canon and Authority: Essays in Old Testament Religion and Theology*. Edited by George W. Coats and Burke O. Long, 42–55. Philadelphia: Fortress Press, 1977.

Coggins, Richard, Anthony Phillips, and Michael Knibb, editors. *Israel's Prophetic Traditions: Essays in Honour of Peter Ackroyd*. Cambridge: Cambridge Univ. Press, 1982.

Collins, Terence. *The Mantle of Elijah: The Redaction Criticism of the Prophetical Books*. Sheffield: JSOT Press, 1993.

Culley, Robert C., and Thomas W. Overholt, editors. *Semeia 21: Anthropological Perspectives on Old Testament Prophecy*. Atlanta: Society of Biblical Literature, 1982.

Darr, Katheryn Pfisterer. "Literary Perspectives on Prophetic Literature." In *Old Testament Interpretation: Past, Present, and Future. Essays in Honor of Gene M. Tucker*. Edited by James Luther Mays et al., 127–43. Nashville: Abingdon, 1995.

Dempsey, Carol J. *The Prophets: A Liberation-Critical Reading*. Minneapolis: Fortress Press, 2000.

Floyd, Michael H. *Minor Prophets: Part 2*. Forms of the Old Testament Literature 22. Grand Rapids: Eerdmans, 2000.

Gitay, Yehoshua. "The Individual versus the Institution: The Prophet versus His Book." In *Religion and the Reconstruction of Civil Society: Papers from the Founding Congress of the South African Academy of Religion, January 1994*. Edited by J. W. de Gruchy and S. Martin. Miscellania Congregalia 51. Pretoria: Univ. of South Africa Press, 1995.

———, editor. *Prophecy and Prophets: The Diversity of Contemporary Issues in Scholarship*. Society of Biblical Literature Semeia Series. Atlanta: Scholars Press, 1997.

Gordon, Robert P., editor. *The Place Is Too Small for Us: The Israelite*

Prophets in Recent Scholarship. Sources for Biblical and Theological Study 5. Winona Lake, Ind.: Eisenbrauns, 1995.

Gottwald, Norman K. "The Biblical Prophetic Critique of Political Economy: Its Ground and Import." In *The Hebrew Bible in Its Social World and in Ours,* 349–64. Society of Biblical Literature Semeia Series. Atlanta: Scholars Press, 1993.

———. "Were the 'Radical' Prophets Also 'Cultic' Prophets?" In *The Hebrew Bible in Its Social World and in Ours,* 111–17.

Gowan, Donald E. *Theology of the Prophetic Books: The Death and Resurrection of Israel.* Louisville: Westminster John Knox, 1998.

Grabbe, Lester L. *Priests, Prophets, Diviners, Sages: A Socio-Historical Study of Religious Specialists in Ancient Israel.* Valley Forge, Pa.: Trinity Press International, 1995.

Gunkel, Hermann. "The Israelite Prophecy from the Time of Amos." In *Twentieth Century Theology in the Making.* Edited by Jaroslav Pelikan, 48–75. New York: Harper & Row, 1969.

———. "The Prophets: Oral and Written." In *Water for a Thirsty Land: Israelite Literature and Religion.* Edited by K. C. Hanson, 85–133. Fortress Classics in Biblical Studies. Minneapolis: Fortress Press, 2001.

Hanson, Paul D. *The Dawn of Apocalyptic: The Historical and Sociological Roots of Jewish Apocalyptic Eschatology.* Rev. ed. Philadelphia: Fortress Press, 1979.

Hutton, Rodney R. *Charisma and Authority in Israelite Society.* Minneapolis: Fortress Press, 1994.

Koch, Klaus. *The Prophets.* Translated by Margaret Kohl. 2 vols. Philadelphia: Fortress Press, 1983–84.

Lang, Bernhard. *Monotheism and the Prophetic Minority: An Essay in Biblical History and Sociology.* Social World of Biblical Antiquity 1. Sheffield: Almond, 1983.

Lindblom, Johannes. *Prophecy in Ancient Israel.* Philadelphia: Fortress Press, 1973.

Long, Burke O. "Prophetic Authority as Social Reality." In *Canon and Authority: Essays in Old Testament Religion and Theology.* Edited by George W. Coats and Burke O. Long, 3–20. Philadelphia: Fortress Press, 1977.

March, W. Eugene. "Prophecy." In *Old Testament Form Criticism.* Edited by John H. Hayes, 141–77. Trinity University Monograph Series in Religion 2. San Antonio: Trinity Univ. Press, 1974.

Miller, Patrick D. "The World and Message of the Prophets: Biblical Prophecy in Its Context." In *Old Testament Interpretation: Past, Present, and Future. Essays in Honor of Gene M. Tucker.* Edited by James Luther Mays et al., 97–112. Nashville: Abingdon, 1995.

Moor, Johannes C. de, editor. *The Elusive Prophet: The Prophet as a Historical Person, Literary Character and Anonymous Artist.* Oudtestamentische Studiën 45. Leiden: Brill, 2001.

Mowinckel, Sigmund. *The Spirit and the Word: Prophecy and Tradition in Ancient Israel.* Edited by K. C. Hanson. Fortress Classics in Biblical Studies. Minneapolis: Fortress Press, 2002.

Nissinen, Martti, ed. *Prophecy in its Ancient Near Eastern Context. Mesopotamian, Biblical and Arabian Perspectives.* Atlanta: Society of Biblical Literature, 2000.

Nogalski, James D. Literary Precursors to the Book of the Twelve. *Beihefte zur Zeitschrift für die alttestamentliche Wissenschaft* 217. Berlin: de Gruyter, 1993.

———. Redactional Processes in the Book of the Twelve. *Beihefte zur Zeitschrift für die alttestamentliche Wissenschaft* 218. Berlin: de Gruyter, 1993.

Nogalski, James D., and Marvin A. Sweeney, editors. *Reading and Hearing the Book of the Twelve.* Society of Biblical Literature Symposium Series 15. Atlanta: Society of Biblical Literature, 2000.

Overholt, Thomas W. *Channels of Prophecy: The Social Dynamics of Prophetic Activity.* Minneapolis: Fortress Press, 1989.

———. *Prophecy in Cross-Cultural Perspective.* Society of Biblical Literature Sources for Biblical Study 17. Atlanta: Scholars Press, 1986.

Parker, Simon B. "Possession Trance and Prophecy in Pre-exilic Israel." *Vetus Testamentum* 28 (1978) 271–85.

Peckham, Brian. *History and Prophecy: The Development of Late Judean Literary Tradition.* Anchor Bible Reference Library. New York: Doubleday, 1993.

Peterson, David L. *The Roles of Israel's Prophets.* Journal for the Study of the Old Testament Supplement 17. Sheffield: JSOT Press, 1981.

————, editor. *Prophecy in Israel: Search for an Identity.* Issues in Religion and Theology 10. Philadelphia: Fortress Press, 1987.

Rad, Gerhard, von. *Old Testament Theology.* Vol. 2: *The Theology of Israel's Prophetic Traditions.* Translated by D. M. G. Stalker. Edinburgh: Oliver & Boyd, 1965. Reprinted Old Testament Library. Louisville: Westminster John Knox, 2001.

Stacey, W. D. *Prophetic Drama in the Old Testament.* London: Epworth, 1990.

Stansell, Gary. *Micah and Isaiah: A Form and Tradition Historical Comparison.* Society of Biblical Literature Dissertation Series 85. Atlanta: Scholars Press, 1988.

Steck, Odil Hannes. *The Prophetic Books and Their Theological Witness.* Translated by James D. Nogalski. St. Louis: Chalice, 2000.

Sweeney, Marvin A. "Formation and Form in Prophetic Literature." In *Old Testament Interpretation: Past, Present, and Future. Essays in Honor of Gene M. Tucker.* Edited by James Luther Mays et al., 113–26. Nashville: Abingdon, 1995.

————. *Isaiah 1–39; with an Introduction to Prophetic Literature.* Forms of the Old Testament Literature 16. Grand Rapids: Eerdmans, 1996.

————. *Twelve Prophets.* 2 vols. Edited by David W. Cotter. Berit Olam. Collegeville, Minn.: Liturgical, 2000.

Tucker, Gene M. "Prophecy and Prophetic Literature." In *The Hebrew Bible and Its Modern Interpreters.* Edited by Douglas A. Knight and Gene M. Tucker, 325–68. Philadelphia: Fortress Press, 1985.

Zimmerli, Walther. *The Fiery Throne: The Prophets and Old Testament Theology.* Edited by K. C. Hanson. Fortress Classics in Biblical Studies. Minneapolis: Fortress Press, 2003.